THE ESSENTIAL INTERNET

Developments in Clinical Psychiatry

A Series of Books Edited By

Anthony L. LaBruzza, M.D.

The books in this series address various facets of the role of psychiatry in the modern world.

Using DSM-IV: *A Clinician's Guide to Psychiatric Diagnosis*
Anthony L. LaBruzza and José M. Méndez-Villarrubia

Filicide: *The Murder, Humiliation, Mutilation, Denigration, and Abandonment of Children by Parents*
Arnaldo Rascovsky

Return from Madness: *Psychotherapy with People Taking the New Antipsychotic Medications and Emerging from Severe, Lifelong, and Disabling Schizophrenia*
Kathleen Degen and Ellen Nasper

Chambers of Memory: *Vietnam in the Lives of US Combat Veterans with PTSD*
H. William Chalsma

Winning Cooperation from Your Child! *A Comprehensive Method to Stop Defiant and Aggressive Behavior in Children*
Kenneth Wenning

Brainstorms: *Understanding and Treating the Emotional Storms of ADHD and Related Disorders*
H. Joseph Horacek

Twisted: *Inside the Mind of a Drug Addict*
Carl Adam Richmond

The Essential Internet:
A Guide for Psychotherapists and Other Mental Health Professionals
Anthony L. LaBruzza

The Essential Internet

A Guide for Psychotherapists and Other Mental Health Professionals

Anthony L. LaBruzza, M.D.

with an Introduction by Howard Benditsky, Ph.D.

JASON ARONSON INC.
Northvale, New Jersey
London

TRADEMARKS

Trademarked names appear throughout this book. In lieu of listing the names and entities that run the trademarks or listing a trademark symbol with each mention of a trademarked name, the author and publisher state that they are using the names for instructional and editorial purposes and to the benefit of the trademark owner with no intention of infringing on that trademark.

Director of Editorial Production: Robert D. Hack

This book was set in 10½ pt. Century Old Style by Alpha Graphics of Pittsfield, New Hampshire.

10 9 8 7 6 5 4 3 2 1

Library of Congress Cataloging-in-Publication Data

LaBruzza, Anthony L.

The essential internet : a guide for psychotherapists and other mental health professionals / by Anthony L. LaBruzza ; with an introduction by Howard Benditsky.

p. cm.

Includes bibliographical references and index.

ISBN 0-7657-0105-7 (alk. paper)

1. Psychiatry—Computer network resources. 2. Internet (Computer network). 3. Mental health—Computer network resources. I. Title.

RC437.2.L33 1997

004.67'8'024616—dc21 97-17194

Printed in the United States of America on acid-free paper. For information and catalog write to Jason Aronson Inc., 230 Livingston Street, Northvale, New Jersey 07647-1731. Or visit our website: http://www.aronson.com

To Stephen Fleck, M.D.,
beloved teacher and colleague,
for his enduring contributions to our profession

CONTENTS

Acknowledgments ix

Preface xi

Introduction by Howard Benditsky, Ph.D. xiii

1 Why Get Connected to the Internet? 1

2 Yin and Yang, Data Transfer, Modems, and Viruses 19

3 The History and Structure of the Internet 27

4 E-Mail, Mailing Lists, and Newsgroups 45

5 Traditional Tools of the Internet—FTP, Archie, Gopher-Veronica-Jughead, Telnet, WAIS, Whois, Finger, and Ping 63

6 The World Wide Web 77

7 Directory of Useful Internet Sites 99

Glossary of Internet and Computer Terms 165

Bibliography 189

Index 191

About the Author 203

ACKNOWLEDGMENTS

This book reflects the input of many friends and colleagues who read the manuscript and offered helpful comments and suggestions. Michael Moskowitz of Jason Aronson, Inc., suggested the idea of writing a book about the Internet especially geared toward psychotherapists and mental health professionals. At first I resisted because of the amount of work it would entail, but later I came to see the wisdom in his suggestion. Paul Falzer contributed his expertise in computer science and countless hours of his time. Linda Podd checked the text for clarity of expression and contributed to improving its general readability. Howard Benditsky wrote the introduction, in which he shares with readers his extensive experience as a clinical psychologist who uses the Internet. Hertz Nazaire directed me to several valuable Web sites that I never would have found on my own. I wish to thank these people and the many others who gave so generously of their time, ideas, and interest in this project.

PREFACE

This book is designed to acquaint psychotherapists and mental health professionals with the essential know-how to access the resources of the Internet and the World Wide Web. I have tried to introduce enough material to make the reader conversant with the major concepts without getting bogged down in technical trivia. Nonetheless, a certain amount of technical knowledge is necessary to make optimum use of the Internet.

The problem with writing a book of this type is deciding which level of computer sophistication to address. Some readers will find almost any book about computers too technical and forbidding. Others will find anything but the most technically advanced treatise a bore. I have made the assumption that the reader has some fundamental knowledge about computers—like how to turn one on and how to use a basic word processor. Yet I am aware that there will be some readers who don't know that once you type in the address of a Web page, you must press the Enter key to make something happen. Or there will be the person who searches in vain for the slot on the computer to insert the paper copy of the letter to be faxed.

In this preface, I will give a brief overview of the book and some basic advice for getting started. First, when you buy a new computer, be sure that it includes a modem, CD-ROM, and a sound card. Don't buy a lot of fancy software because most of what you need can be downloaded for free directly from the Internet. Find out from a friend about a good Internet service in your local area. Contact that service and gauge its quality by how quickly they get you up and running. Be sure you can cancel the contract without too much expense if you find the service unsuitable. A service that provides busy signals most of the time is of little value when you want to connect to the Internet.

If you are as yet unfamiliar with the Internet, you need to know that it is simply a very large (worldwide) network of computers that are electronically connected to share information. Anyone with a home computer, a modem, and the proper software can enroll with an Internet service provider to connect his or her own computer to this worldwide network via the telephone line. Joining the Internet community gives you access to the information on all the other Internet-linked computers in the world.

The Internet has many tools for finding the information you want on this worldwide network of computers. Some of these tools predate the World Wide Web and have strange names like Gopher, Veronica, FTP, Telnet, and so on. The most popular method for sharing information on the Internet, however, is the World Wide Web, which consists of millions of electronic "pages" linked to one another by "hypertext links" that let you jump effortlessly from page to page through Webspace. These terms may look unfamiliar, but you will understand them by the time you finish this text.

I have made every effort to keep the explanations plain and simple. On occasion I have repeated definitions and technical material in different chapters to make the reading as effortless as possible. Whenever possible, I have provided URL addresses to Web sites that provide additional information—the best way to learn is by doing. In addition, there is a glossary of the most common Internet terms for easy reference. Browsing the glossary is a quick way to become acquainted with Internet terminology. My hope is that this book will enable you quickly and efficiently to join your colleagues who already appreciate the value of the Internet in their daily and professional lives.

INTRODUCTION

GETTING CAUGHT UP IN THE NET

HOWARD BENDITSKY, PH.D.

Tony LaBruzza's book on the Internet is a gift. It provides a concise yet explicit and eminently accessible guide that brings an oftentimes apparently impenetrable maze into sharp focus. This book is a kind of map to that maze, locating the strategic pathways and doors, describing what is to be found behind them, and even giving reasons for visiting. It provides the basic tools necessary to enter the maze and return with whatever treasure for which you might be searching. Written in a simple and direct style, this text at once reflects both the author's ability to make very complex topics understandable and his ability, as a teacher, to convey information at a pace that readers of this book will find easy to integrate. It is a class on the Internet and Dr. LaBruzza is the professor.

In computing days of the early 1980s there was a game entitled *Adventure*. This game, which might have been played on an IBM computer with an 8-bit processor (today's Pentiums are 32-bit processors) and a monochrome screen, took you on a treasure hunt through an entirely nongraphic (verbally formatted) maze. The object was to gain points by locating and retrieving various treasures while outwitting or destroying the monsters that protect the treasure without getting yourself lost in the process. The game was played by asking questions in a specific format and giving the computer the directions (left, right, straight, up, down) as to which way you wished to go. Frequently you had no idea where you were and would have to physically sketch the maze in order to orient yourself, as well as to return to where you were if you wished to return to the game the next day. If we liken this maze to the much more complex maze that is the Internet, this book provides a map of that maze. After reading this book you will have an understanding of the various components of the Internet, their purpose, how to access them, and how to use them effectively to accomplish your goals.

In the remainder of this introduction I would like to provide you with an idea of how I have used the Internet for both personal and professional enhancement. In addition, I will provide two examples of how the Internet has been beneficial to specific patients with whose cases I am quite familiar.

I first began to use the Internet about 5 years ago. At that time I was using an IBM clone computer with an Intel 386 megahertz (mhz) processor, 4 megabytes (megs) of random access memory (RAM) and a 120 megabyte hard drive. My modem had a top speed of 1200 baud and I subscribed to one of the large online service providers, who offered Internet access as one of its features. Currently I am using a computer with a 90 mhz Intel Pentium processor with 16 megs of RAM and a 1 gigabyte (1 billion bytes of information) hard drive. I now subscribe to one of the large online service providers that provides only Internet access and do so via a 56K faxmodem (capable of sending and receiving both e-mail and faxes). This modem theoretically allows me to communicate with the Internet at an information transfer rate of 56 kilobytes per second, faster than any phone line currently available for this purpose.

When I first got "on line" (connected to the online service provider and through it to the Internet), I had visions of the movie *War Games* in my head. Since then I have settled for more pedestrian, and legal, uses. I use the Internet for several personal purposes. Through e-mail (electronic mail) I keep in touch with family and friends who are spread across Canada and the United States. E-mail allows me to contact them almost instantly and have a response back just as quickly. All this happens for the cost of a local phone call and the price of the monthly connection to my current online service provider ($9.95 for 10 hours of unrestricted access per month, and beyond 10 hours $2.50 an hour). In addition, I engage in interactive chat groups (like a phone call with several parties on the line simultaneously except communication is via type as opposed to voice) with people throughout the world who are interested in topics that also interest me. I can also check my stock portfolio and watch the performance of other stocks in which I am considering investing. When I need to travel I can research various destinations, price airline tickets, and, if I choose, make reservations and purchase tickets. I can also check what's playing at the local theaters, and download free software from various sources.

For example, I recently visited the Microsoft Web page and downloaded a patch kit that repairs known bugs in the current version of Windows 95. At the same time I downloaded a program that protects my Microsoft Word files from the "macro" viruses. I also recently contacted the Web page of the New School for Social Research in New York (**http://www.dialnasa.edu/home.html**), in order to see whether, among the online courses they offer, there was one on Visual C++, a programming language I am trying to learn. Besides these activities I can access reviews of various plays, purchase books, play computer games, and collect information on topics that vary from the most pedestrian to the more arcane.

There are also various newsgroups to which I subscribe (at no cost) to keep in touch with other people throughout the country with whom I share common interests. Here I find a collection of letters and responses on various aspects of the subjects that interest me. I can just browse the information submitted by others or post (submit for view by all others visiting the news group) my questions or observations. For example, I am interested in the Japanese art of bonsai (dwarfing trees) so I am in touch with a bonsai news group (**http://www.rec.acts.bonsai**). I am also interested in photography and darkroom work (**http://www.rec.photo.darkroom** and **http://www.rec.photo.advanced**). A third news group that proved quite helpful was one concerned with car problems (**http://www.rec.auto.tech**). Here I was able to post questions and receive suggestions concerning problems I was having with my car.

On the topic of cars, if you have ever planned to buy or sell a car and consulted the "Blue Book" to obtain an unbiased estimate of how much you should pay for your new car or, conversely, how much you should ask for your old car, the Internet is a real timesaver. For me, this had always involved a trip to the library to consult the "Blue Book." Not any more. I can now consult the "Blue Book" web page (**http://www.kbb.com/**) and get the prices without leaving home. Finally, if you have adolescents going off to college, try contacting College Link (**http://www.collegelink.com/**) for information on the college of your choice.

The Internet is also extremely valuable from a professional perspective. For example, through membership in Medscape (**http://www.medscape.com/default.html**), I can access and search the MedLine database for all the current articles on topics of interest to me. They also send me a newsletter each week that, among other things, features articles, the full text of which can be downloaded or printed. All of this information is available without cost.

Through the Internet, I can also contact the American Psychological Association and communicate with various departments directly, obtain the latest information in the profession, view or print articles from the *American Psychologist*, or access their employment opportunities section. Similar Web pages authored by the National Academy of Neuropsychology (**http://libertynet.org/~nan/**) or the American Medical Association (**http://www.ama-assn.org/**) are also available online.

Another interesting Internet application concerns the ability to access information on topics you have heard about. For example, about two years ago I read an article in the *New York Times* (also available online at no charge) about a project designed to make available via computer the MRI (magnetic resonance images), CAT (computerized axial tomography) scan, and gross dissection images of a prisoner who had donated his body for this purpose. As my particular interest is in neuropsychology, I was particularly interested in the neuroanatomical aspects of this project. Through the Internet (**http://www.uke.uni-hamburg.de/institutes/mdm/idv/visiblehuman.html**) I was able to locate a site that provided information, both written and graphic, about "Voxel Man," view the type of information that was available and learn where and how I could purchase software that integrates the information I wanted into a very sophisticated neuroanatomical atlas available on CD-ROM.

Through various newsgroups it is also possible to keep up with or participate in discussions on a variety of topics from pharmacology (**http://www.sci.med.pharmacy**) to the public's concerns with anxiety and panic (**http://www.alt.support.anxiety-panic**). There are also a variety of national and international informal chat groups in which you can participate interactively on a variety of topics.

Finally, I would like to provide you with two brief examples of instances where patients derived clinical benefit from the use of the Internet. The first case is a married white male in his 40s who had been in psychotherapy in the past for quite some time for a variety of symptoms including a chronic low-grade depression, anxiety, and obsessive-compulsive traits. He had discontinued treatment after some time, feeling much improved. Years later, after experiencing a traumatic event, he returned to psychotherapy, this time with symptoms of a major depression. After some preliminary sessions he decided to consulted a psychiatrist, who recommended a trial of Zoloft, 50 mg daily. The patient complied with this recommendation but found after a week that he could not tolerate one of the side effects of this medication (in his case, an exacerbation of his anxiety and insomnia). A initial attempt to switch him to Prozac, 10 mg daily, had even more pronounced side effects. It was about this time that the patient, who was in contact with an Internet support group on depression (**http://www.alt.support.depression**), read a posting by a man who had a similar reaction to Zoloft. He also learned that this man had overcome this problem by dividing the 50 mg dose into quarters and titrating upward from 12.5 mg to 50 mg of Zoloft, increasing the dose by 12.5 mg each week. The patient tried this regimen and at the end of a month was up to 50 mg (25 mg twice a day), experiencing no side effects, and getting a full antidepressant effect.

The second case concerns a married white male in his 30s who was rather introverted and reserved and had considerable difficulty expressing his feelings, except when he exploded verbally at his wife and family in response to even minor frustrations. Despite months of psychotherapy he was unable to effectively be in contact with and express how he felt. However, through the therapy, despite never really achieving any meaningful insight into his feelings or their origins, he was able to learn to identify the signs of his growing frustration and remove himself from the source of frustration prior to his exploding. When he returned to therapy a year later in response to marital difficulties, it was astounding to see how much more effective he had become at expressing his feelings. Inquiry as to how this had come about revealed that he had purchased a computer and struck upon the idea of sending e-mail to his wife. He had found that in contrast to his verbal output, when sitting at the keyboard he was able to be much more articulate in expressing his thoughts and feelings, and as he did so (and received supportive feedback from his wife also via e-mail, as well as directly) he found himself becoming more in touch with himself and developing an emotional vocabulary that led him to become more adept at communicating face to face with others. This process of communicating by e-mail with his wife then expanded to communicating with strangers, via a chat group, which further enhanced his communication skills and generalized his ability to express himself. The process also had the unexpected outcome of causing him to become interested (for the first time) in the self-help books his wife often read. Through this process, facilitated by his growing contact with his own feelings, he was able to identify with what he read, seeing much of himself in these books, and thereby deepening his insight into himself and others.

The book you are about to read will take you through the complexities that comprise the Internet. In simple direct language, it will provide you with the understanding and tools necessary to "surf" (access and move about) the Net (Internet). Unlike real surfing, when surfing the Net you never have to wait for the right wave.

1 WHY GET CONNECTED TO THE INTERNET?

Mental health professionals sometimes experience anxiety at the thought of logging on to the Internet. Unfortunately, the more they avoid plunging into cyberspace, the more they are likely to feel left behind. Today's reality is that to be computer illiterate is to function as an intellectual dinosaur. This book is intended to assist computer-phobic professionals to face reality, confront their avoidance, and begin to experience the rewards and pleasures of computer-assisted living.

Learning a few basic concepts and two dozen new words can turn even the most inexperienced user into a seasoned surfer of the World Wide Web. Just a short while after starting to use the Internet, people usually wonder how they ever did without it. If you're absolutely new to cyberspace, you will need to know that the Internet is simply a worldwide network of computers linked together to share information. The collection of all the networked computers and their connecting cables and telephone lines resembles a giant fisherman's net or spider's web that envelopes the globe. With a modem and the proper software, you can connect your home computer to this huge network and communicate with any other linked computer in the world.

In 1996 I traveled to Nicaragua as a member of a delegation on domestic violence. Logging on to the World Wide Web (a central part of the Internet), I was able to locate Web sites that contained information about the local weather, news, politics, and conditions in Managua and León, Nicaragua—the two cities I planned to visit. Using e-mail (electronic mail), I was able to correspond instantaneously with mental health professionals in Nicaragua. This was much faster than sending letters by "snail mail" (land and air) and much cheaper than making international phone calls. In addition, by including their Internet addresses in the carbon copy or CC: section of the e-mail, I was able to send copies of my messages to the other members of the delegation to keep them abreast of the plans.

Part of the delegation included attendance at the March 1996 Central American Psychiatric Congress in Managua, where I was invited to give a paper comparing the diagnosis of Posttraumatic Stress Disorder in the *DSM-IV* and the *ICD-10*. Again, using the Internet, I was able to research the international literature, find relevant articles, check government statistics on domestic violence, correspond with international experts, and send copies of the early drafts of my paper via the Internet to colleagues for their comments and suggestions. The availability of these resources on my home computer saved countless hours and numerous trips to the library.

Doing the research for this book provided yet another example of the usefulness of the Internet. Because technology is advancing so rapidly, the Internet is constantly changing and developing. Fortunately, it is possible to find current information about almost any topic by searching the Internet. Throughout this text, I will refer the reader back to the Internet for further information. Be aware, however, that new Internet sites appear and older ones disappear daily. Some sites move to a new host computer and change their addresses, and others go out of existence completely.

The remainder of this chapter will list some of the potential uses and benefits of the Internet for mental health professionals. Don't be frightened if you come across some unusual terminology, because these topics will be further elaborated later in this book. In the next chapter we will review how computers process information and come to a better understanding of what the Internet is and how it works.

E-MAIL

E-mail, or electronic mail, allows you to send and receive messages to anyone in the world who also has a computer that can receive e-mail. Estimates are that the Internet currently processes about 30 million e-mail messages daily. Unless Internet traffic is particularly heavy, this process takes place almost instantaneously and is a great improvement over paper mail in the postal service ("snail mail"). In addition, most e-mail software allows you to encode and attach files to your e-mail documents. You can send an encoded article, computer program, picture, sound file, or video clip to colleagues anywhere that you can send e-mail.

One dentist on the East Coast, for example, connected his video camera to his personal computer to take videos of dental x-rays that he wanted to send to a colleague in California for a second opinion. Using his video software, the dentist converted a videotaped frame of the x-ray to a computer file, which he then attached to the e-mail describing the case. His colleague was able to respond after reading the description of the case and viewing the x-ray on his home computer in California.

The President of the United States and most members of Congress maintain e-mail sites to receive comments from their constituents. If you have a legal complaint, you can often send e-mail to your state attorney general or consumer protection agency. There is a site for documenting your experiences with the abuses perpetrated by managed care companies. No doubt, you will find e-mail to be one of the most useful features of the Internet.

The recent development of "smart phones" allows users to access e-mail via the telephone. With a smart phone, business executives can now retrieve their messages via a cellular or hard-wired phone by simply entering a code and listening to the messages (Sweeney 1996). Computer users can use telephone e-mail technology by installing the necessary software (e.g., E-mail Reader by Millennia Software) to get e-mail access on the road via an ordinary phone call to the home or office computer through its voice-capable modem.

CHATS

The Internet has areas that are devoted to electronic chats. You simply connect to an area of interest and type what you have to say in the space provided. When you press the Enter key on your keyboard, your message appears in the chat box next to your name. Other people who are participating in the chat will respond in writing, and the chat will go on. Most online services like Prodigy and America Online provide chat rooms to their members. There are also freestanding chat areas, like WBS or the WebChat Broadcasting System, that sponsor both public and private chat rooms and even allow you to create a free home page. The Internet address or URL (Uniform Resource Locator) of WebChat is **http://www.wbs.net/** and its Web page (accessed here through the AOL Web browser) looks like this:

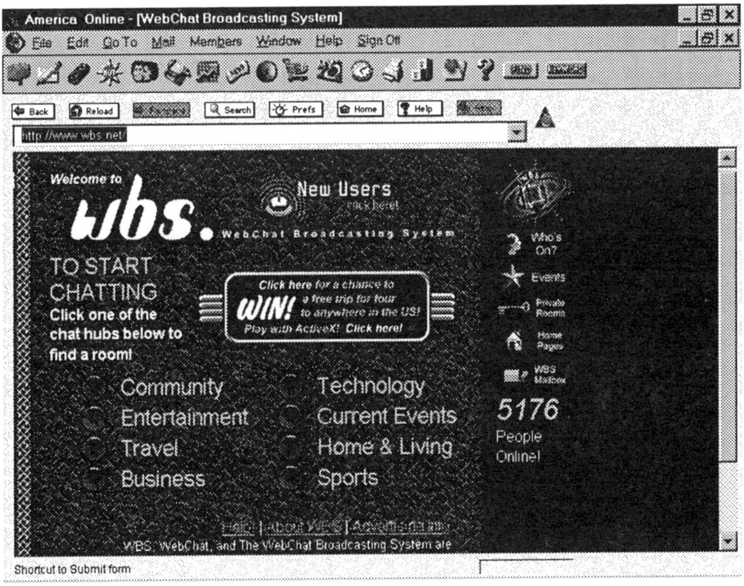

INTERNET RELAY CHAT (IRC): THE NEW CB RADIO

A Finnish computer whiz, Jarkko Oikarinen, invented a method for people around the globe to communicate with one another simultaneously on the Internet. Oikarinen's method is called Internet Relay Chat, but everyone refers to it as IRC. Sometimes thousands of computer users worldwide are online simultaneously in the same chat! Internet Relay Chat became quite popular during the United States Gulf War with Iraq when computer users around the world followed the events of the war in online IRC chat rooms as those events were actually happening. Just as with a CB radio, users choose a "handle" (code name) for the chat. Jarkko Oikarinen goes by the handle Wiz. You connect to IRC channels through an IRC server. The addresses of two public access servers mentioned on the Internet are:

telnet://sci.dixie.edu:6677
telnet://vinson.ecn.uoknor.edu:6677

Unfortunately, there is no guarantee that these sites will remain open indefinitely.

If interested in IRC chats, you may find the mIRC home page helpful. Its Web address is **http://www.mirc.co.uk/index.html**. According to mIRC, "to connect to IRC you'll need a small chat program like mIRC. mIRC is the shareware IRC chat program made for Windows by Khaled Mardam-Bey. It offers a fast and clean interface to IRC and it is well equipped with options and tools. You can download mIRC for free!"

NEWSGROUPS OR USENET NEWSGROUPS

Newsgroups are public areas on Usenet (the Users Network) that are similar to both chats and e-mail. Each newsgroup is a discussion group devoted to a particular topic. Usenet is simply a network of computers that exchange databases of discussion-group articles with one another. The articles are catalogued by topic into the various newsgroups. Members subscribe to a newsgroup via e-mail and then receive public e-mail about the topic as it is sent to the group. Members can read the newsgroup's e-mail and respond if they desire. Newsgroups that are made up of experts in a field can be enlightening and provide answers to difficult questions.

COMMERCIAL NEWS—ALL THE NEWS THAT'S FIT TO SURF

If you are interested in traditional news, the commercial online services and many Internet sites provide the day's top news stories, weather, sports events, soap opera updates, and so on. For starters, you might try the following URLs on the Web:

CBS: **http://www.cbs.com**
CNN: **http://www.cnn.com/**
ESPN: **http://espnet.sportszone.com/**
MSNBC: **http://www.msnbc.com/**
NBC: **http://www.nbc.com/**
New York Times: **http://www.nytimes.com/**
USA Today: **http://www.usatoday.com**
Wall Street Journal headlines: **http://info.wsj.com/headlines/**

If you prefer not to read but rather to hear the news, try CNET radio on the Web. Its URL is **http://www.news.com/Radio/Rams/1997/02/20/ns.ram**. Yes, you can actually listen to your computer as if it were a radio. The most popular method for delivering sound clips via modem is a program called RealAudio, which is available as a free add-on to the two major Web browsers, Netscape Navigator and Microsoft Internet Explorer. RealAudio is available on the Web at **http://www.cmihub.com/info/news/raudio.htm** or at **http://browserwatch.iworld.com/plug-in.html**. There is also a commercial software program called WebStereo that brings Internet Radio from around the world to your home computer. For information about WebStereo, contact Insanely Great Software (126 Calvert Ave. E., Edison, NJ 08820) at their home page on the Web at **http://www.igsnet.com** (where you can download a shareware copy for a 30-day free trial), at phone 800-319-5107, or fax 908-632-1766.

VOICE AND VIDEO CONFERENCING

With the right equipment (a full duplex modem, sound card, and video camera) and the proper software (e.g., NetMeeting and Microsoft Internet Browser, or CoolTalk and Netscape Navigator), you can connect to colleagues around the world for live conversations, including a video of the person with whom you are speaking. The cost of this service is the price of a local phone call that connects you to your Internet provider. Phone companies are upset by this development and are lobbying to be able to charge users for local Internet access. Needless to say, many Internet users are not happy with the greed displayed by the telephone companies. I recently received the following e-mail message from the Microsoft Network (MSN) in my e-mail box:

> Date: Fri, 7 Feb 1997 13:44:11 -0800 (PST)
> From: MCN Business Manager **<mcn@mcn.org>**
> Subject: Per minute charges on phone lines filed with the FCC
>
> The FCC is currently reviewing a matter which may directly affect you, an MCN customer and Internet user. I'm forwarding you the following message for your information. You may also wish to read the Reuters news article at:
>
> **http://www.news.com/News/Item/0,4,7723,4000.html?latest**
>
> "Hi from Tim (Badge) on IRC Cops. I am writing you this to inform you of a very important matter currently under review

by the FCC. Your local telephone company has filed a proposal with the FCC to impose per minute charges for your Internet service. They contend that your usage has or will hinder the operation of the telephone network. It is our belief that Internet usage will diminish if users were required to pay additional per minute charges. The FCC has created an e-mail box for your comments; responses must be received by February 13, 1997. Send your comments to **isp@fcc.gov** and tell them what you think. Every phone company is in on this one, and they are trying to sneak it in just under the wire for litigation."

Please send e-mail to the following address clearly stating your opinion about this issue: **isp@fcc.gov**

Rennie Innis, MCN Business Manager

By the time this book goes to press, the issue of whether we end-users will have to pay more to the phone company for local calls to our Internet providers may already have been decided.

DOWNLOADING AND UPDATING FILES AND PROGRAMS

The Internet makes available thousands of computer programs that are either free (freeware) or to be tested prior to purchase if you like them (shareware). Many of these sites are sponsored by universities and government agencies. Excellent shareware sites where you can download (receive via modem) software include Shareware at **http://www.shareware.com/**, Winsite at **http://www.winsite.com/**, and Tucows at **http://tucows.myriad.net/acc95.html**. In addition, most software manufacturers sponsor sites where you can download the latest revisions or updates of commercial software that you own either for free or for a modest update fee. There is even a commercial program (Oil Change by CyberMedia; WWW address at **http://www.cybermedia.com/**) that, on its own, will search the

Internet and then download and install any updates to the programs on your hard disk.

You can also download text files that contain information about virtually anything; for example, one site has the entire text of the Unabomber's lengthy manifesto. Sites that make files available for you to download are referred to as FTP sites because your computer uses a program (set of computer instructions) called the file transfer protocol to look through and copy the files that are stored on the other computer (FTP site). If you plan to download, you will need to protect your computer from viruses, those nasty little programs that infect and damage your files.

FAXING ON THE INTERNET

It is now possible to send documents via e-mail that will then be faxed to companies or individuals residing a local phone call away from the host computer. This method of faxing can save money, especially if you need to fax regularly to foreign countries. Some commercial sites offer low-cost faxing services for a fee that is far below what the telephone company would charge. If you don't know the fax number of a company, the Internet provides directories of fax and voice phone numbers around the world.

Not long ago I was looking for a particular computer program developed by a software company in Ecuador. I had the name of the program and of the company but could not locate its address, Web site, or e-mail address. Through a search of the Web, I discovered a site sponsored by the commerce department of Ecuador which offered free faxes to Ecuadorian commercial locations. Using this free fax offer, I sent my request for information and a few days later I received e-mail from the company in Ecuador answering my questions about their program.

LITERATURE, LIBRARY, AND DATABASE SEARCHES

For professionals, the Internet provides the ability to search databases like MedLine for the most recent articles on a topic, and many of these databases are free. Physicians can look up medication effects and drug interactions. Students and writers can search library card catalogues for bibliographical references. Computer users can tap into government statistics and information centers. Patients can find information about their disorders and participate in self-help groups online. Some libraries offer the entire texts of books and journals online. No matter what your area of interest, you are likely to be able to research it in cyberspace.

CONTINUING EDUCATION

Many sites offer tutorials and some universities offer courses for credit on the Internet. *Newsweek* (1997) reported that Duke, Ohio University, and Purdue are offering M.B.A. degrees via classes on the Internet. It is possible for physicians to read or listen to case discussions and receive CME credit (for example, Medical Matrix at **http://www.slackinc.com/matrix/**). You can find lists of professional meetings and places to obtain educational material for patients. There are also some excellent Internet tutorials. In case you don't want to read this book, try Jack Nelson's Internet Tutor at **http://www.i-tutor.com/**. While you're at it, check out Ohio State University's Internet Tutor at **http://gateway.lib.ohio-state.edu/tutor/instructions.html**. Another excellent overview of the Internet is EFF's Extended Guide to the Internet at **http://www.eff.org/papers/eegtti/eeg_toc.html**.

PHONE DIRECTORIES AND MISSING PERSONS

Many sites on the Web offer national telephone directories, zip code assistance, or help finding people with whom you have lost touch. If you get an urge to locate an old college classmate, you might be able to find him or her via the Internet.

A valuable site is Database America's People Finder, whose URL is **http://www.databaseamerica.com/html/gpfind.htm**. Using this database, you can enter the name or telephone number of someone and it will search for their U.S. address and zip code. If you want to find all your relatives in the United States, just do a search on your last name. You will find many other sites containing directories, search engines, white pages, and yellow pages in the directory section of this text.

ELECTRONIC BILLING AND TRANSFER OF PATIENT INFORMATION

Most insurance companies allow office practices to bill for services via the telephone line connected to a computer. This can save clinician's time in receiving payment and the cost of postage for paper claims. Many hospitals are moving to electronic patient records that doctors with a valid password will be able to access from their home computers. Because of the need to maintain confidentially of electronically transmitted materials (patient records, credit card numbers, government secrets, and so on), many methods of encryption have been developed. For a discussion of Phil Zimmerman's Pretty Good Privacy utility, set your browser to **http://www.ifi.uio.no/pgp/pgp.shtml**, where you will see a page that begins with the quote:

> PGP (short for Pretty Good Privacy) is a highly secure public key encryption program originally written by Philip Zimmermann. Over the past few years, PGP has got thousands of ad-

herent supporters all over the globe and has become a de-facto standard for encryption of e-mail on the Internet. If you don't know whether PGP is something for you, please take some time to read Phil Zimmermann's article on why you should use PGP.

YOUR OWN HOME PAGE ON THE WEB

The World Wide Web is the central and fastest growing part of the Internet. You can jump from page to page on the Web by following a series of hypertext links related to the topic that interests you. Most Internet providers allow clients space on the host computer to store their personal Web pages. You can devote your Web page to an area of personal concern or use it to advertise your services. For example, a college student who suffers from sickle cell disease decided to launch a Web site to provide information and encouragement to other sickle cell sufferers. Check out his page at the Web address **http://www.angelfire.com/az/nazaire/index.html** on the World Wide Web.

To use the above address, just copy it exactly as it appears here into the Web page address slot (or document URL box) on your Web browser (the program you use to access the World Wide Web) and press the Enter key on your keyboard. We will review exactly what such an address signifies in a later chapter. Note that many computers speak a language called UNIX that is *case sensitive*, meaning that it makes a difference whether you type a word in capital or small letters. Always copy a Web address (URL or Uniform Resource Locator) exactly as it is written, taking note to preserve the upper and lower case letters.

Many online services offer free home pages and include instructions for using their online editor to help you design your page. Three popular Web sites that offer a free home page are:

http://www.angelfire.com/
http://www.geocities.com/
http://wbs.net/

SURFING THE WEB

As mentioned above, the World Wide Web has pages dedicated to almost any topic you can imagine. Modern Web browsers like Mosaic, Netscape Navigator, and Microsoft Internet Explorer make surfing the Web child's play. You can find information about almost any topic somewhere on the Web.

SHOPPING AND TRAVEL PLANNING

When the going gets tough, the tough go shopping. Is it any surprise that consumers have turned the Web into a giant electronic shopping mall? Professionals can find books and equipment to buy. Some clinicians are even offering counseling and psychotherapy via the Internet.

If you are planning a trip, you can research the history and geography of the place you plan to visit. You can check airline schedules and then make reservations for flights right from your home computer. Many hotels offer sites that help you locate and reserve hotel rooms. Hotels tend to have rather obvious addresses on the Web like **http://www.hilton.com** and **http://www.holiday-inn.com**.

BANKING AND FINANCE

Many banks and most investment firms make available electronic financial services. From your home computer you can check your accounts, pay bills, transfer money, buy and sell stocks, get historical stock information, and so on. Some commercial financial software programs (e.g., Quicken, Microsoft Money, etc.) can take the information from your bank or investment firm and give you a clearer picture of your financial situation. Internet security is obviously an important issue for financial transmissions on the Net.

JOB HUNTING

For those who are looking to find a new job or change careers, the Web has pages devoted to job hunting. It is possible to read classified ads from newspapers around the country. Some companies allow you to submit your resume via modem from your home computer, and there are even reports of employers interviewing prospective employees online in special chat rooms.

FUN AND ENTERTAINMENT—INTERNET ADDICTION?

For many the Internet is simply great fun. You can find almost any kind of entertainment in cyberspace including such diverse items as the ever popular pornographic sites, interactive games, 3-D virtual realities, live chats, and your daily horoscope. There is talk of people becoming addicted to surfing the Web, spending all their free time at the computers. Spouses occasionally complain that they see very little of their partners since the arrival of the personal computer in the home. Perhaps Internet Abuse and Dependence will become new diagnostic categories in the next version of the DSM.

Not to worry. The Internet offers its own support group for those who can't keep their hands off the keyboard. To subscribe to the Internet Addiction Support Group, simply e-mail the address: **listserv@netcom.com**, leave the subject line of your e-mail blank, and for the body text of the message write: subscribe i-a-s-g.

PORNOGRAPHY, CENSORSHIP, AND PARANOIA ON THE WEB

Because anyone with a computer can get onto the Internet, it should be no surprise that a significant number of social deviants lurk in cyberspace. Some of them plant computer viruses, others send hate mail or sponsor truly revolting newsgroups and Web pages. An African-American colleague, for example, told me that his African-American Web chats are frequently interrupted by members of the KKK who go there to taunt its participants with racial slurs.

Parents are concerned, with reason, because young children with an Internet connection can access pornographic and other materials that are prohibited to them by law. Furthermore, in chat rooms children can befriend people of questionable character. One mother grew concerned when a man who was detained in a local prison called to make a date with her teenage daughter. Cases have appeared in the news of pedophiles and rapists meeting their unsuspecting victims over the Internet.

More than any other communications medium, the Internet highlights the issues that surround the fundamental American freedom of speech, the very foundation of our democracy. Recall that the First Amendment to our Constitution states: "Congress shall make no law respecting an establishment of religion, or prohibiting the free exercise thereof; or abridging the freedom of speech, or the press; or the right of the people peaceably to assemble, and to petition the government for a redress of grievances." Unfortunately, the U.S. Congress has passed a law, the Exon/Gorton Communications Decency Act of 1996, to limit free speech on the Internet. This law may be in violation of the First

Amendment and at the time this book was being written, the Exon/Gorton Act was being reviewed by the United States Supreme Court. I can only hope that by the time this book goes to print, the Act will have been declared unconstitutional by our highest court.

According to the Communications Decency Act, "Whoever . . . initiates the transmission of any comment, request, suggestion, proposal, image, or other communication which is obscene, lewd, lascivious, filthy . . . shall be fined under title 18, United States Code, or imprisoned not more than two years, or both." The problem is that our current conservative and most ethical Congress has defined what is indecent. Under this act, it is illegal to discuss abortion or breast feeding on the Internet because the act defines abortion and breasts (and any explicit description of sex) as obscene. Doctors may not transmit via the Internet photos of genital lesions that can be found in any dermatology textbook. Art history teachers would face arrest if they displayed a photo of Michelangelo's David (a naked youth) at their Web site. For further examples, see the page whose URL is **http://box.hotwired.net/banned.html**. This law is now being challenged in the courts. The complete text of the act can be found on the Web at **http://www.cpsr.org/cpsr/nii/cyber-rights/web/cda/cda.final.html**.

Because cyberspace mirrors our society, there will of course be pornography and offensive material on the Internet. Anti-American, antidemocratic legislation like the Exon/Gorton Act is not the solution if we wish to remain a free society. Fortunately, the Internet itself is addressing these problems. Check out the HateWatch page at **http://hatewatch.org/**. Parents can purchase special censorship software (like Cyber Patrol, which offers a free demo at **http://www.cyberpatrol.com** or Gulliver's Guardian at **http://gulliver.nb.ca**) that will block their child's access to sites that use words and phrases deemed offensive by the parents. Employers can use similar software to keep employees from surfing to unacceptable or pornographic Web sites on company time.

Before leaving the topic of paranoia, I should mention that some Internet veterans are suspicious of Bill Gates and his monopolistic tendencies. Microsoft has made access to its own Microsoft Network (MSN) a part of Windows 95, and according to Kennedy (1995), "many commentators suspect that Microsoft intends its network eventually to supersede the Internet" (p. 40). Some computer users also fear that when they connect to online services or register programs by modem, the computer on the other end is gathering information about their computer and software without their knowledge or consent—a violation of privacy. Finally, there is evidence in news reports of government lawsuits against individual citizens that a certain amount of government eavesdropping is taking place on our Internet communications.

« « « UPDATE « « «

As this book was going to press, the United States Supreme Court declared that the Internet should have the same First Amendment protection as books and newspapers, in contrast to the more limited protection afforded broadcast media and cable television. According to the front page article of *The New York Times* of Friday, June 27, 1997:

"In a sweeping endorsement of free speech on the Internet, the Supreme Court today declared unconstitutional a Federal law making it a crime to send or display 'indecent' material on line in a way available to minors. The decision, unanimous in most respects, marked the Court's first effort to extend the principles of the First Amendment into cyberspace and to confront the nature of a new, and—to most of the Justices—an unfamiliar medium."

2 YIN AND YANG, DATA TRANSFER, MODEMS, AND VIRUSES

In the previous chapter we considered some of the reasons why mental health and other professionals would want to connect to the Internet. In this chapter we will take a look at how computers process information in preparation for better understanding the functioning of the Internet. When you finish reading this chapter, you won't be a member of the "digerati" (the digital communications equivalent of the literati), but you will have a basic idea of how computers chop up (digitalize) and manipulate information.

THE YIN AND YANG OF COMPUTER DATA MANIPULATION

Ancient Chinese philosophy holds that all things can be analyzed into two basic factors, yin and yang. In 1689 the philosopher Gottfried Wilhelm von Leibniz (1646–1716), who developed the system of binary arithmetic that computers use today, received a copy of the Chinese *Book of Changes* (*I Ching*). The book was sent by a Jesuit missionary, Father Bouvet, who was familiar with Leibnitz's work and noticed the similarity between Leibnitz's binary arithmetic and the 64 Chinese hexagrams (sequences of six lines that could represent either yin or yang).

Leibnitz saw immediately that the 64 *I Ching* hexagrams were binary representations of the 64 integers from 0 to 63 in the standard decimal system. In his 1703 treatise on binary numbers, Leibnitz credited their origin to the ancient Chinese philosopher Fuxi, legendary author of the *I Ching*. According to Huang and Huang (1987), Leibniz believed that "God has revealed the truth to Fuxi three thousand years before his time" (p. 41).

Computers apply the Chinese philosophy of yin and yang to electrical circuits. In computerese, *data* refers to any kind of information handled by the computer. Being machines, computers can deal only with *binary bits* of information. In a process called *digitalization*, computers break down words, pictures (graphics), and sounds into simple but lengthy sequences of 0s and 1s. This is similar to the Morse code of early telegraphy, which transforms the letters of words into sequences of long and short tones. In our Chinese analogy, computers transform all data to sequences of yins (0s) and yangs (1s), the *bits* or (b)inary dig(its) of data processing. Such sequences are easy to manipulate by electronic circuits. For example, a picture can be broken down into a sequence of binary bits by one computer. That sequence can then be sent electronically to another computer, which then transforms the sequence of bits into its original, humanly recognizable form.

Computers communicate by sending streams of binary or digital information (bits, 0s and 1s, yins and yangs) back and forth via wires, fiber optic cables, or satellite transmissions. Most readers will be connecting with other computers via their telephone lines. Unfortunately for computers, telephones were designed to transmit human voice (analog communication) rather than digital information. To solve the problem that phone lines pose for computers, engineers developed devices to transform digital information into analog (voice-like) signals that can be sent over phone lines. A similar device at the receiving end takes the analog signals from the telephone line and converts them back to digital signals that the computer can understand. Such devices are called *modems*, short for MOdulator/DEModulator. Modems modulate digital data, converting it to analog signals that can travel over phone lines, and then demodulate the analog signal, converting it back to computer-friendly digital sequences on the receiving end.

To connect one computer to another by modem, you simply dial the phone number of the other computer just as you would call a friend. The modems then do a "handshake" to be sure they recognize each other (to humans this sounds like hisses, pings, and bongs in the modem's speaker). If the handshake is successful, communication begins. Modems vary in how fast they can process data. The *baud rate* of a modem indicates how many digital bits it can transmit per second (abbreviated as bps).

For Internet access, faster is better. A 14.4 baud modem is barely adequate to meet the demands of graphic transmissions on the Internet. The minimal standard is rapidly becoming 28.8 baud, and faster modems are constantly appearing on the market. When purchasing a system for Internet use, it is advisable to buy the fastest modem you can afford and hope that the phone company will catch up with the speed of your modem. In reality the current telephone system infrastructure does not support the fastest modems available, and it is rare that even a 28.8 baud modem can connect to the Internet via a home phone line at a rate faster than 26.4 bps.

Most ordinary end-users (folks who use computers) will connect via modem, but modems have their drawbacks. When traffic is heavy on the "infobahn" (named after the autobahn in Germany) or "information superhighway," transmission of data, especially of graphics, can slow to a snail's pace. Businesses and power-hungry "net junkies" yearn for more speedy transmissions. Currently, there are three main alternatives to modems for those who are not limited by either money or availability of services. These are ISDN, cable modems, and xDSL.

Integrated Services Digital Networks (ISDN) replace the modem with a special digital phone line that connects your computer via an ISDN adapter to the Internet service, thus making transmission of data two to four times faster. Eventually the rapid ISDN technology will replace our current much slower analog telephone system. Some cable TV companies offer cable modems that can theoretically speed transmission up to 350 times that of a standard 28.8 baud modem. Finally, xDSL refers to Digital Subscriber Lines that were originally developed to offer subscribers video on demand, but the technology is now being developed to offer high-speed Internet access. Over the next several years improvements in the telephone infrastructure (such as high-speed fiber optic cables or even satellite communications) may eventually retire the current generation of modems to the junk heap.

CHOOSING A MODEM

Because most readers will be using a modem, let's spend some time reviewing the types of modems available. Modems can be classified into four broad categories, each with its own advantages and disadvantages. These are internal modems, external modems, PCMCIA, and portable or pocket battery-operated modems.

Most desktop computer systems come with internal modems already installed. Internal modems have the advantage of being out of sight, less expensive than external modems, and not occupying a serial port that can be used to connect other devices to the computer. Some disadvantages of internal modems are that they are not portable and that they occupy an internal slot that cannot then be used to install other cards inside the computer. In addition, modems sometimes “freeze” or “lock up” the computer in the midst of an online session, and internal modems cannot easily be turned off the way that external modems can.

External modems are more expensive than their equivalent internal counterparts. They are also visible, bulkier, and may take up valuable desk space. External modems plug into a serial, parallel, or SCSI port that may then not be available for other devices. If a modem plugs into a serial port, that port must be able to transfer data fast enough to accommodate the modem or it will have to be replaced with a faster serial port. External modems have the advantages of being portable and of having an external power switch that can be used to turn off the modem should it “freeze” the computer during an online session.

PCMCIA and portable modems have the advantage of being extremely small, light, and easily portable. PCMCIA modems were designed for notebook computers and fit into a special PCMCIA slot on the computer. Portable modems connect, like external modems, to a serial port. They can operate on battery power, which makes them easy to use on the road. Unfortunately, they tend to be rather expensive to purchase, and the use of batteries can make them expensive to operate. Another risk is that the batteries may run out of power at crucial moments. International travelers will need to check whether the country they are visiting supports the type of power and telephone line connections required by the modem.

In addition to data transmission, most modern modems offer fax and voice capabilities. In fact, many computer users allow their modem to replace their telephone answering machine. Modems can distinguish the type of signal on the phone line, that is, whether it is voice, fax, or digital computer data, and then route the signal to the proper channel.

ELECTRICAL FLUCTUATIONS AND COMPUTER VIRUSES

Because telephone lines and electrical power lines are subject to fluctuations in electrical current and to bursts of electrical energy (or even lightning strikes), I strongly recommend a surge protection device for both the computer and the telephone line that plugs into the modem. If you live in an area that has power brownouts, it would be wise to invest in a battery backup to protect your computer equipment from damage due to electrical power loss. There are several reputable companies, like American Power Supply (on the Web at **http://www.apcc.com**), that make these devices and include a warranty to replace the cost of your equipment should it suffer from electrical damage while properly connected to their surge protector or battery backup.

Another danger to your computer that may arrive by way of modem is the dreaded computer virus. A virus is simply a small computer program that can damage your files or even erase your hard disk. Like their biological counterparts, computer viruses can replicate themselves. They can also infect and alter other programs, often in a destructive manner. Most viruses are small, allowing them to be quickly and easily transferred to your computer from a floppy disk or via a modem connected to a computer network. Viruses often lurk in the boot or system sectors of floppy or hard disks, just waiting to be transferred when the computer is booted up from an infected disk.

To do their dirty work, viruses must infect and act within programs that perform some function in the computer. Thus, viruses do not transfer via word processing files, which are simply displays of text, but viruses typically do infect command or executable files (the ones that end in ".exe" or ".com"). An exception is a virus that can infect a Microsoft Word document though its ability to execute macros, which are like little programs within the word processing document. Fortunately, Microsoft is aware of this problem and has offered a solution that is available for downloading from its Web site at **http://microsoft.com/MSWordSupport/Content/usage/MacroVirus/default.htm**. Here is what Microsoft has to say about this particular virus on its Web page:

> A macro virus is a new type of virus that uses a program's own macro programming language to distribute itself. Unlike previous ("traditional") viruses, macro viruses do not infect programs; they infect documents. . . .
>
> Microsoft has identified a particular macro virus, dubbed the Prank Macro, or Concept Virus. This is a harmless but annoying macro. . . .
>
> The Prank Macro is characterized by: a dialog box that appears when you open an affected document; files that are changed to templates without your knowledge; and certain macros that are installed in Word.
>
> Microsoft is aware of other macro viruses that affect Word documents. The best defense against any of these is to install anti-virus software specifically designed to detect macro viruses.

Any computer user who downloads files via modem or brings home a floppy disk from the office should invest in virus protection software. Just as humans bring home colds or the flu that they caught from co-workers, computer disks that come home from the work site are notorious carriers of computer viruses. Most of the commercial anti-virus programs have Web sites that allow users to download the latest virus definitions and thus keep their software up to date. In addition, there are shareware (programs you can test and purchase only if you decide to use them) and freeware (no cost) anti-virus programs available on the Web. The better programs have a ***memory resident*** feature that allows them to work continuously in the background, checking all new arrivals for evidence of viral infection.

In addition to running anti-virus software, another useful preventive measure is to make a backup of all important files just in case your hard disk crashes or gets damaged by a viral invasion. Always keep a rescue disk handy—it's better than Prozac if you suffer a hard disk crash, a truly depressing experience. Windows 95 has a built-in option for creating a rescue disk that contains all the essential files needed to boot your computer should the hard disk fail to operate. Once you make a bootable rescue disk, be sure to enable its write-protection feature so that it cannot be erased, infected, or modified.

When you download files via modem, be sure you know the source. Most software companies maintain Internet sites for both advertising and upgrade purposes. Because their reputations are at stake, these companies keep their sites free of viruses. In addition there are many well-established file transfer protocol (FTP) sites that make files available. For more information about viruses on the Internet, check out the WWW Anti-Virus Update Center at: **http://www.crl.com/%7Ecolocomp/novirus2.htm**.

3 THE HISTORY AND STRUCTURE OF THE INTERNET

In the previous chapter we learned that computers digitize all types of information into strings of 0s and 1s (binary bits) and communicate with one another by sending these binary strings back and forth over phone lines, optic cables, or beamed satellite transmissions. When two or more computers are connected in a way that allows them to share digital information, they form a local *network* of computers, and we call this back-and-forth sharing of electronic information among computers *internetworking*. The global network that links together the thousands of local networks of computers is called the *Internet*. When you connect to the Internet, your computer links to an extensive wide-area network (WAN) that allows you to share information (internetwork) with any of the millions of computers that are also connected worldwide. In short, as a network of networks, the Internet is the largest electronic computer network in the world.

THE ORIGINS OF THE INTERNET

It would not be farfetched to attribute the inspiration for the Internet to Soviet leader Nikita Khrushchev. Under Khrushchev's leadership, the Soviet Union developed a hydrogen bomb and in 1957 launched the first satellite, Sputnik, into space. Out of fear, paranoia, and a desire to restore its wounded national pride, the United States formed the Advanced Research Projects Agency (ARPA) to catch up with the Russians and try to keep the U.S. technologically ahead of foreign powers. The scientists at ARPA seized upon *packet-switching technology*, an idea proposed in 1962 as a way for computers of any type to be able to communicate and share resources with one another.

The idea behind packet-switching technology is simple and elegant. Because computer data is simply long strings of 0s and 1s, those strings can be broken into small pieces or packets, much as an entire book can be parceled into individual paragraphs. These small packets are easier and safer to transmit than very large ones. Each small piece of string (or paragraph, to use that analogy) can be labeled with an address, indicating where it is to go and in what order it is to be reassembled. The small packets can travel by different routes to their destination. If one route is busy or unavailable, the packets can be redirected along a different pathway to reach their destination.

The model for this type of transmission is the fisherman's net or the spider's web. Rather than sending information along a single continuous path that can easily be broken, the packet-switching method allows pieces of information to travel from one part of the web or net to any other along any available route. If the Soviets were to nuke or destroy one of the computers in the network, the packets of information could take alternate routes to reach the other computers in the net—just as a spider can take many routes to reach the prey that gets caught in its web. When all the pieces of string (or paragraphs) arrive at their destination, the receiving computer can reconnect them into their original form. The instructions that tell the computer how to address and disassemble data into packets and then reassemble those packets into the original data are called an *internetworking protocol* (IP), and each packet of data is given a label that directs it to a computer at a particular IP address.

For obvious reasons, this packet-switching idea was appealing to the military, and in 1969 Bolt, Beranek, and Newman developed an experimental packet-switching network, referred to as ARPANet, for the United States Department of Defense. The purpose of ARPANet was to share information among the computers of various types owned by the university, military, and defense contractors who were working on projects for ARPA. Other universities, government agencies, and businesses were impressed with the success of the ARPANet and wanted to get in on the action. As a result, in 1973, ARPA, which had then been renamed DARPA (the Defense Advanced Research Projects Agency) began an Internetting Project whose goal was to form a network of packet-switching networks, thus making packet-switching IP technology more widely available to the computer-using community. In 1973 Great Britain and Norway joined the network. As more and more computer networks joined the system, this network of networks evolved into the Internet as we know it today.

OTHER KEY DATES IN INTERNET HISTORY:

For the sake of brevity, I will list some other important landmarks in the development of the current Internet system:

1972: The microprocessor is invented, making the personal computer possible.

1972: Electronic mail (e-mail) is first used on mainframe computers.

1976: Steve Jobs builds the first Apple computer.

1979: Newsgroups are started by Usenet (the User's Network).

1980: IBM introduces its first PC (personal computer).

1981: Mailing lists are developed by BITNET.

1989: The World Wide Web (WWW) comes into existence.

1990: The original ARPANet is phased out of existence.

1991: GOPHER (a program that searches for information on the Internet) and WAIS (not a psychological test, but a Wide Area Information Server that searches the Internet for specific text) come into being.

1993: MOSAIC (a Web browser program that allows you to browse or surf the Web) arrives on the scene, making the World Wide Web immensely popular.

1994: Microsoft launches Windows 95, which includes the Microsoft Network with access to the Internet built directly into the Windows shell.

1995: The major online providers (CompuServe, America Online, Prodigy, Microsoft Network) make Internet access universally available.

1996: In November, America Online offers unlimited Internet access for $19.95 a month and suffers horrendous traffic jams on its connections to the Internet.

1997: In January about six million computers are connected to the Internet, and the figure seems to be doubling annually.

IP ADDRESSES, TCP/IP, DOMAIN NAMES, AND E-MAIL ADDRESSES

The *internet protocol* (IP) sets the standard for providing addresses for the small packets of data that travel over the Internet. Just as each house in America has a unique street address, each computer that is permanently connected to the Internet has a unique IP address that is 32 bits (thirty-two 0s and 1s) long. Without these unique IP addresses, the billions of packets of information that travel the Internet would not know where to get off.

A companion protocol, the *transmission control protocol* (TCP) defines the standards for how computers disassemble data into smaller packets, label those packets with addresses and reassembly instructions, and reassemble those packets into the original data when they reach their destination. TCP also checks to be sure that all the packets of data have arrived in good condition. If a packet has been damaged in transit, TCP sends a request to the computer of origin requesting a fresh copy. Because they work closely together, we usually refer to these two protocols with the single term TCP/IP and we talk about internetworking with TCP/IP as the basis of the Internet.

How do the little packets of data know where to go? Computers called *routers* link the various networks that make up the Internet. These routing computers figure out the most efficient route to send the small data packets. The TCP protocol neatly tucks the data packets into little addressed "envelopes" and sends them to computers at the proper IP addresses. In essence, routers act like a central post office that sorts pieces of mail and directs them to the proper destination.

Because humans use the decimal system rather than the computer's binary arithmetic (0s and 1s), IP addresses appear on the Internet as strings of four numbers separated by dots or periods ("dotted quads"). For example, the computer that hosts Angelfire, a service that provides free home pages, has the IP address 207.226.241.14, and the Angelfire service has the Web address **http://207.226.241.14/**.

Fortunately, it is unnecessary to use the numeric IP address of a computer on the Net because most computers also have *domain names*, that is, identifying labels written as letters, words, abbreviations, and acronyms rather than numbers. In English, the above IP address 207.226.241.14 becomes **http://www.Angelfire.com/**. This address tells us that the Angelfire service can be found on the World Wide Web (www) and is a commercial (com) enterprise. Most domain names clearly identify the host computer and are easy to remember; for example, the address of *The New York Times* on the World Wide Web is **http://www.nytimes.com**.

E-mail is usually addressed by attaching the person's computer name (user id) with the symbol @ (at) to the domain name of the Internet host and looks like this: **YourName@Computer DomainName**. For example, I have an account with the Physician's OnLine Network whose domain name is pol.net. Since I use my last name as my user id on POL (Physician's OnLine), my e-mail address there becomes **LaBruzza@pol.net**.

Feel free to write to me at **LaBruzza@pol.net** with comments or suggestions about future editions of this book, but please no flaming, spamming, or SHOUTING. Flaming is done by "flamers," who try to light a flame under the reader by sending repugnant or provocative messages. Spamming is named after the canned food with a similar name and refers to the sending of irrelevant messages of low nutritive value. To SHOUT is to WRITE EVERYTHING IN CAPITAL LETTERS. The problem is that SHOUTING makes your message harder to read and is considered boorish behavior on the Net. When in Rome, do as the Romans do; when on the Net, follows the rules of Netiquette (Net etiquette).

For practice, here are some other e-mail addresses. They all have the form **UserName@ComputerDomainName**. See if you can figure out who or what they refer to:

ask-a-geologist@usgs.gov
billg@microsoft.com
cancernet@icicb.nci.nih.gov
DaveLaBruzza@bigfoot.com (Hint: David is my son)
president@whitehouse.com

Many domain names end in letter codes separated by periods. These codes indicate the domain type (educational, commercial, military, etc.) and the state or country of origin (Colorado, France, Japan, España, etc.). For example, there is a file transfer protocol (FTP) site at the Universidad de los Andes (University of the Andes, abbreviated Uniandes) in Colombia, South America. The domain name address of this Internet site is **ftp://gopher.uniandes.edu.co/** and we see from this address that "uniandes" is an educational institution (edu) located in Colombia (co).

Country codes appear at the very end of the domain name and often consist of the first two letters of the country's name as it is spelled in that country's native language. Country codes are sometimes omitted, especially for U.S. sites, but a state code may then be included. For example, David Clark, the author of the *Student's Guide to the Internet*, lists as his e-mail address **clarkd@bvsd.k12.co.us**. In this example, "bvsd" signifies the computer; "k12," the network; "co," Colorado; and "us," the United States. Some common country codes are:

ar	Argentina	hk	Hong Kong
au	Australia	il	Israel
br	Brazil	in	India
ca	Canada	it	Italy
ch	Switzerland	jp	Japan
cl	Chile	kr	South Korea
cn	China	mx	Mexico
co	Colombia, South America	nl	Netherlands
de	Germany (Deutchland)	no	Norway
dk	Denmark	pe	Peru
ec	Ecuador	se	Sweden
es	Spain (España)	su	Russia
fi	Finland	tw	Taiwan
fr	France	uk	United Kingdom
gr	Greece	ve	Venezuela

Codes for the type of domain appear at the end of the domain name, just before the country code if one is included. Some common codes for types of domains include:

ac	academic (UK)
com	commercial organization or company
co	commercial organization or company in UK
edu	educational institution
gov	governmental
mil	military
net	Internet host or gateway
org	nonprofit organization

URL ADDRESSES ON THE WWW

While we're on the subject of the Internet's domain name system or DNS (everything in cyberspace has an acronym), let's review the uniform resource locator (URL) addresses used by the World Wide Web (www). The Web consists of a giant collection of Web pages all linked together by means of hypertext or hypermedia links. By clicking with your mouse on such a link, you can go to the next page in the series. A single Web page in New York may link to pages stored on computers in London, Cairo, or anywhere in the world. Each Web page has a unique address, namely its URL or uniform resource locator.

For example, here is the Web address (URL) of the Anti-Virus Update Center: **http://www.crl.com/%7Ecolocomp/novirus2.htm**. Notice that, like all Web page addresses, this URL begins with **http://**, which stands for the hypertext transfer protocol, the method used to read pages on the Web. Following the **http://** comes the name of the computer, most often in domain name language. In this example the computer is identified as **www.crl.com.** A forward slash (/) separates the computer's domain name from the next entry, which in this case is the folder or directory in the computer labeled **%7Ecolocomp**. Finally, another forward slash (/) separates the name of the folder from the name of the file **novirus2.htm** whose contents will appear on your screen when you go to that site.

Not all Web page addresses (URLs) contain names of directories (folders) or files. Often a URL simply indicates the computer's domain name (or sometimes the computer's numerical dotted quad name). Domain name URLs are usually descriptive of the organization providing the Web site. Examples include **http://www.microsoft.com/** (Bill Gates's company), **http://**

www.aronson.com/ (the publisher of this book, so be sure to visit this site and order lots of books), **http://www.i-tutor.com/** (home of an excellent Internet tutorial), and **http://www. datatrackinc.com/** (a company that designs Web pages using the latest technology—check this out for its state of the art graphics and animation). Here is an illustration of what happens when you enter a URL in your Web browser (Microsoft Internet Explorer in this example) using the URL **http://www. aronson.com:**

The same principles apply to foreign language locations like the Spanish Web site of Web search engines and maps whose URL is **http://www.intercom.es/navegador/busca.htm**. Here the computer is identified as **www.intercom.es** (es for España or Spain), the folder is **navegador** (navigator), and the file is **busca.htm** (*busca* meaning "search" in htm or hypertext format).

SUMMARY OF INTERNET UNIFORM RESOURCE LOCATOR (URL) ADDRESSES

URLs are also used for sites on the Internet other than the World Wide Web. To summarize, a URL generally has the form "Protocol://DomainName/Directory/FileName" and consists of:

1) an abbreviation of the Internet protocol (the instructions used to exchange data). Such protocols include *http* (the Web's hypertext transfer protocol), *ftp* (the file transfer protocol), *gopher* for Gopher sites, and so on.
2) a colon (:) usually followed by two forward slashes (//) because the WWW uses UNIX operating system's forward slashes (//) rather than the DOS operating system's backward slash (\). An exception is Usenet, which omits the two forward slashes (//) and simply employs the word "news" followed by a colon (:) and then the name of the newsgroup. For example, to read the newsgroup entitled "alt.obituaries" you would type "news:alt.obituaries" in the URL field of your browser. If your interests are more prurient than death, you could enter "news.alt.sex" in the URL locator.
3) the computer's address (domain name), followed by a forward slash (/).
4) the name of the directory path on the host computer, followed by a forward slash (/).
5) the name of the particular file that you are looking for in that directory (folder).
6) for WWW pages, the suffixes *.html* or *.htm*, which stand for the hypertext markup language used by the Web.

CLIENTS, HOSTS, SERVERS, AND INTERNET SERVICE PROVIDERS

You, the client, must connect to a *server* or *host* computer to log onto the Internet. The server computer acts like a host in welcoming you and your computer to the Net. The term *server* also refers to the software program that provides you with the host/server computer's services (e.g., e-mail, WWW access). Your computer must run its own client software to connect to a welcoming host computer. Once you are connected, the host computer allows you access to its server software, thus providing you with various services like e-mail, the World Wide Web, Gopher, Usenet groups, chats, and so on. World Wide Web browsers like Netscape and Microsoft Internet Explorer are among the most popular pieces of client software.

Internet service providers (ISPs), or Internet access providers (IAPs), are companies that, for a fee, allow you access to their computers so that you too can connect to the Internet. In addition, the popular online services like CompuServe, Prodigy, America Online, and Microsoft Network will lease you access, usually for a monthly fee, to both the Internet and their own private commercial networks, which offer proprietary services not available to nonsubscribers. Connection to an Internet service provider or to an online service is usually via a local telephone call and costs no more than the monthly service fees to the Internet provider and to the telephone company. As a result, sending messages around the world on the Internet does not incur any long-distance charges. As mentioned previously, telephone companies are lobbying to charge extra for local calls to Internet providers.

Let's review briefly what happens when your home computer connects to a service provider's host computer. Using its client software, your computer is able to get onto the Net through the host computer's server software. Recall that the host computer has a direct line to the Internet. When you send a request to connect to a site on the Net, your message passes from your computer through the host computer and onto the Net. This process is carefully regulated by special computers called *routers* that stand, like traffic cops, between the host computer and the rest of the Net. The router directs traffic by taking the information from the host and deciding on the most efficient method to send it to its destination. Packets of information usually pass through many routers via high-speed T1 and T3 computer lines before they get where they are going. You don't need to know any of this to use the Net, but it is kind of interesting. You will, however, need to set up an account with a service provider before you can access the Net.

Be careful when choosing a commercial online service or an internet provider. If they require long-distance telephone access, you will run up huge phone bills. If they suddenly get busy you may not be able to connect at times that are important for you. Let me illustrate with my personal tale of woe. In December 1996 America Online (AOL) announced unlimited Internet access for only $19.95 per month, and was flooded with new subscribers who were then unable to connect most of the time. The attorneys general of several states threatened AOL with a lawsuit because it was selling a service it was unable to provide. I learned first-hand how frustrating this can be. As a member of AOL, I got busy signals about 95 percent of the times that I tried to connect between December 1996 and March 1997. Between those dates I was writing the final draft of this book and needed to get online frequently to verify information that I was including in the text.

Actually, I switched to AOL when the Microsoft Network (MSN) suddenly decided to eliminate local access numbers in Connecticut beginning December 1996. Despite the fact that I had paid for a year of service only nine months previously, MSN simply eliminated local access and confronted me with the choice of either paying huge long-distance phone bills or else switching to another provider. Despite the inconvenience (e.g., the need to notify everyone of my new AOL e-mail address so I would not miss any messages), I switched from MSN to AOL, out of the frying pan and into the fire. Although AOL was a local call, it was almost always busy. Fortunately, I also belonged to Physicians OnLine, which was seldom busy and allowed Internet access when I needed it. I did write to Microsoft to request a refund on the unused portion of the year's service that I had paid for and that Microsoft had summarily eliminated. Months later, Microsoft's customer service department has still not responded despite the fact that when I first registered with this software giant, I received a response telling me how much my happiness meant to Bill Gates and the folks at Microsoft. It seems that Bill doesn't care about me anymore.

Current AOL users should go to Keyword *autodialer* and download that feature. Autodialer will automatically attempt to connect to AOL nine times for each phone number listed. This automatic retry feature can save AOL users a lot of aggravation.

The best way to find an Internet service provider in your area is to ask for recommendations from colleagues who are already connected to the Internet. If they report bad experiences (like mine with both AOL and MSN), you would be wise to avoid those providers. Be sure the provider has a local access telephone number, and don't be afraid to ask about their average caller-to-modem ratio, that is, the average ratio of service users to the number of available lines provided by the service. A ratio of 10 to 1 is perfectly acceptable, but ratios greater than 12 to 1 suggest you will get busy signals more often than you would like when you try to connect. The industry standard is a caller-to-modem ratio of between 12 and 15 to 1; AOL's ratio in the early months of 1997 was about 33 to 1, more than double the industry average. You can do your own spot check of the caller-to-modem ratio by calling the access line periodically and noting how often you get a busy signal over the course of a week.

Most Internet providers offer client software and technical support free as part of their introductory package. If you have trouble connecting, you don't want to spend a fortune trying to figure out what went wrong. Many providers also allow you to list different names on the same account (a family package). For example, America Online permits several members of a family to use distinct screen names for chats and individualized e-mail addresses. Finally, read your contract and know exactly what you are purchasing and how much it costs.

WAYS TO CONNECT TO THE INTERNET FOR EVERY BUDGET

There are many ways to connect to the Internet ranging from the plain, cheap, and simple to the complex, expensive, and sophisticated. Many high schools and most universities offer their students and faculty Internet access, and many corporations and government agencies make the Internet available at the work site to employees. Those not fortunate enough to have Internet access at school or on the job will have to find a way to connect via their home or portable computer.

The least expensive method to have at least partial Internet access is via a local bulletin board system (BBS) or a freenet system. Local businesses and interest groups often sponsor electronic bulletin boards for free or for a minimal fee. Freenets are community sponsored BBSs that provide information about local events, school calendars, and so on. Such electronic bulletin board systems usually offer e-mail and the ability to chat with other patrons of the BBS. To connect to a BBS, you simply dial its number (usually a local or sometimes a toll-free 800 call) via the communications software that comes with your modem.

With free access to e-mail, you can send messages via the Internet to anyone else in the world with an e-mail address. You can also subscribe to mailing lists, which are discussion groups conducted entirely by e-mail. To subscribe to a mailing list, you simply send e-mail to the address of the mailing list and request that your name and e-mail address be added to the list. Then, every time someone posts a message to the list, you and everyone else on the mailing list will receive a copy of the newly posted message. Some mailing lists are managed by actual people (web masters and web mistresses) and others are managed by a computer program such as listserv.

For example, if you were Jewish and single, you might want to subscribe to the Jewish Singles Mailing List (JSML), a forum for posting personal notices. To get on the list you would send e-mail to the address **zeus@cs.umd.edu** and list as the subject of your e-mail message: JSML. The text of your e-mail message would include your name, age, sex, location, and other personal information that you want to share on the list. Once your message arrives at **zeus@cs.umd.edu**, it is retransmitted to all the other Jewish singles on the list who can then decide if they want to establish personal contact with you.

Those who can afford it will want to have full Internet access by subscribing to either a commercial online service or to an Internet service provider (ISP). The commercial services (America Online, CompuServe, Prodigy, Microsoft Network, etc.) tend to be more expensive than ISPs but they offer proprietary services that are not available to nonsubscribers. In addition, the commercial services are usually simple to install and operate—everything can be done with the click of a mouse. America Online now offers unlimited Internet access for $19.95 per month if you are lucky enough to be able to connect. CompuServe has a literature search of professional journals that is extremely useful if you are writing a paper or doing research.

The Internet service providers (ISPs) have been more complicated to install and set up than the commercial services like AOL, but Windows 95 has made the setup much easier. They have traditionally come with at least three software components: a connection program like Trumpet Winsock, a Web browser like Mosaic or Netscape, and an e-mail program. New ISPs seem to be springing up almost daily and even the telephone companies are getting in on the act. The advantage of services like SprintNet and AT&T WorldNet (as well as commercial services like AOL and CompuServe) is that you can connect locally from anywhere in the United States.

In choosing an ISP, you will also need to consider which type of connection is available: a SLIP, a CSLIP, or a PPP. Don't you just love all these acronyms! A SLIP is a serial line Internet protocol, which is the oldest method of connecting to an ISP. SLIP has a major disadvantage in that it does not check to see if the data arrives on your computer free of transmission errors. A CSLIP is a compressed serial line Internet protocol, which is essentially identical to SLIP except that the data is compressed to increase the rate of transfer of information. A PPP is a point-to-point protocol, which is more recent and more reliable than SLIP because it checks to be sure that data arrives free of transmission errors. PPP also has the advantage of faster transfer rates than SLIP.

A final word of advice on choosing an Internet connection is to consider the cost. Currently many providers offer unlimited access for about $20 per month. Many of the commercial online services and some Internet providers offer a limited number of hours for a basic fee and then charge an hourly rate of $2 or $3 per hour for additional time spent. Read the fine print. If you become an Internet junkie on a fee-per-hour service, you could easily spend $100 or more per month. *Caveat emptor*: let the buyer beware! As an added precaution, you might consider downloading a freeware program to monitor the time spent on the Internet.

If you have Internet access, you can check out a list of Internet providers on the Web page called ISP Finder—"the easy way to find a local service provider" at **http://www.ispfinder.com/**.

4 E-MAIL, MAILING LISTS, AND NEWSGROUPS

The modern World Wide Web (WWW or W3) is the most popular aspect of the Internet and is rapidly supplanting many of the traditional tools of the Internet. Before focusing on the WWW, however, it will be helpful to review the older but still useful features of the Net. Much of this material will be familiar from the earlier sections of this book. Here we will summarize and expand the earlier discussions of these topics. Let's begin with the most widely used feature of the Net, namely, electronic mail or e-mail (also written as E-mail, Email, and email).

E-MAIL

Electronic mail allows the user to send messages instantaneously around the world to anyone who has an e-mail address. Because e-mail consists of text files that are sent over the Internet, it is quicker, easier, and more convenient than paper-based correspondence ("snail mail"). You can attach binary files (e.g., computer programs, images, photos, sound files, video clips) to e-mail text. It is also possible to download FTP files and do Gopher searches via e-mail. FTP and Gopher will be explained later in this chapter.

When you sign up for Internet service, you will be given an Internet e-mail address by your server (host computer). Such addresses consist of your "handle" or account name followed by the symbol @ (at) and then the domain name of your server. As mentioned previously, e-mail addresses have the form **YourName@ComputerDomainName**. We saw that President Clinton's e-mail address is **president@whitehouse.com** and my address on the Physician's OnLine Network is **LaBruzza@pol.net**.

To send e-mail to someone, you must know their e-mail address. The best way to find someone's e-mail address is to ask them. Although there are directories of e-mail addresses on the Net, they are limited in what they contain and you may surf away empty-handed. Many universities have online directories of their faculty and students. For example, you can try the University of Notre Dame's Gopher site **http://gopher.nd.edu**. Once at the gopher root site at that address at Notre Dame, you click on the menu option labeled Non-Notre Dame Information Sources and then choose the menu option Phone Books—Other Institutions for a list of all the directory servers (computers that house address lists) in the world.

You can also get e-mail address information from the Web page entitled CCSO Phonebook Gateway—Server Lookup at **http://www.uiuc.edu/cgi-bin/ph/lookup**. On this Web page you will find a box where you enter the name of the server or host computer whose directory you wish to search. For example, if you wanted to find my address at Yale University, you would enter

Yale as the name of the server and then click Enter on the screen. You will then see a screen labeled CCSO Phonebook Gateway Yale University—directory.yale.edu, where a box appears in which you would enter my last name. Then, pressing Enter again will show you my name, address, e-mail address, and phone number in the Yale University directory.

Yet another way to locate an e-mail address is to get a current copy of the FAQ (frequently asked questions) document entitled "How to Find Someone's Email Address." You can get this information at Web sites **http://www.csi.uottawa.ca/info/how-to-email.html** or at **http://www.pimall.com/nais/n.email find.html**. Other helpful resources of address information are Infoseek's E-mail Directory at **http://www2.infoseek.com/Facts** which claims to have "over 7 million e-mail addresses from around the world" and the WhoWhere? E-mail Addresses page at **http://www.whowhere.com/**.

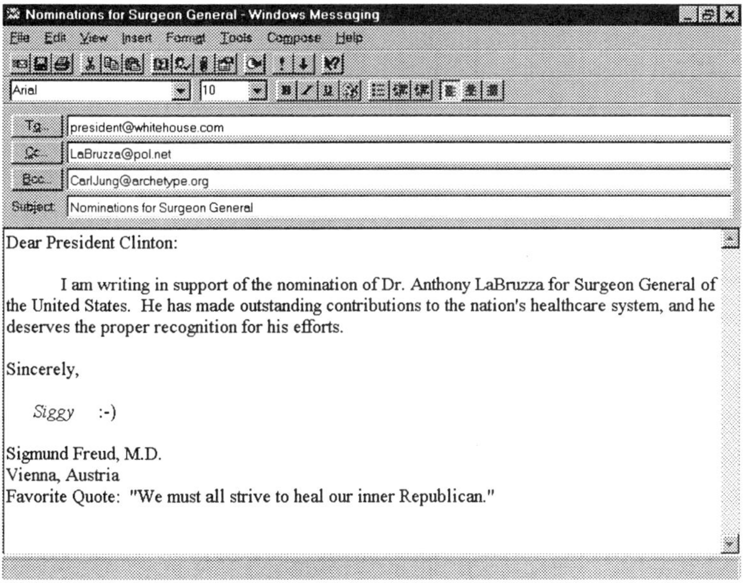

As part of their e-mail package, most Web browsers and e-mail software programs present you with a form that looks like an office memo. You simply complete the sections of the form, click on Send, and your e-mail is on its way through cyberspace. The illustration above shows the e-mail template from Microsoft Windows Messaging.

Let's review how to complete the above form. First, you enter the address of the person to whom you are writing—in this case, President Clinton. Next, if you wish, you can send a carbon copy of the e-mail to someone. Here Dr. Freud sent a carbon copy (Cc) to the author at **LaBruzza@pol.net** and sent a blind carbon copy (Bcc) to his colleague Carl Jung at the fictitious address **CarlJung@archetype.org**. A blind carbon copy allows you to send someone a copy of the message without revealing who else is receiving a copy. In this example, Sigmund Freud did not want Carl Jung to know that he had sent Dr. LaBruzza a copy of the message.

The next field on the form is labeled Subject and allows you to label your correspondence with a relevant title. Below the subject field is the main body of the e-mail where you write the actual text of your message. Beneath the body of the text, some people like to insert a signature file, which is simply a brief series of lines that includes relevant information like your phone number, snail-mail address, a favorite quotation, and perhaps some ASCII (text and characters from the keyboard) art or even smileys or emoticons (emotional icons). ASCII refers to the American Standard Code Information Exchange, which is simply the text generated by your keyboard. The ASCII code is a way of standardizing text to allow data transfer between computer systems.

ASCII art, if you can call it that, is a design created by using the character set on the standard keyboard. For example, you can draw a stick figure that looks something like this:

```
  O
o-----o
   |
  / \
--     --
```

Emoticons are a type of ASCII art, consisting of little figures that look like happy faces or expressions of other emotions. You usually have to turn the page (or your head) sideways to get the picture. For example, a smiling face on its side might look like [: -)] whereas a bout of depression might result in the weeping emoticon [:'- ( ]. Frankly, I find the use of emoticons rather silly, and the mere sight of them brings out the devil in me [}:>]. To see more sophisticated samples of ASCII art, go to Delirium's ASCII Art Collection at **http://www.lsi.usp.br/usp/rod/ascii/ascii.html**.

To summarize, the e-mail template of most Web browsers and e-mail software consists of several fill-in-the-blank sections and components. These include:

To: The e-mail address and/or name of the person or persons to whom you address the message. You can usually include multiple addresses separated by commas. Most software includes an *Address Book* feature that allows you to store names and e-mail addresses that you can simply click on to enter in the To field.

From: The e-mail address and/or name of the sender.

Subject: The descriptive heading or title of the message.

Main Text or Body of the Message: Here's where you write the body of your letter.

Cc: The e-mail address of the person or persons to whom you wish to send a carbon copy.

Bcc: A blind carbon copy is one sent to the e-mail address of a person (or persons) who will not be aware that others have received a copy. Not all e-mail programs offer this feature.

Signature: Many e-mail programs allow you to develop a customized signature that you can place at the end of your message. This might include your name, address, phone number, a promotional quote, and even a scan of your actual written signature.

Attachment: Most e-mail programs allow you to attach a binary file to your text message. Binary files are encoded using a special encoding protocol like MIME or UUencode that may appear as gibberish if the receiver does not have the corresponding decoder. Encoding is discussed in more detail below.

Attaching, Encoding, and Decoding

Had Freud wished to include a file with his e-mail to President Clinton, he would have clicked on the Attach button (depicted as a paper clip beneath the word Format of the menu bar). Clicking on Attach (the paper clip icon) would prompt him to select a file to attach to his message. There is a catch, however, to Attach. Prior to transmission, computers encode binary (non-text) files to enable them to be attached to e-mail messages because e-mail can only transmit ASCII text on the Internet. The value of encoding into ASCII characters and then decoding is that all types of files (word processing, computer programs, graphics, sound, etc.) will arrive at their destinations as exact duplicates of the original files that you sent.

Unfortunately, the encoding protocols are not uniform, and the three most common methods (MIME, UUencode, and Binhex) are all incompatible with one another. As a result, the receiving computer must be able to decode the file from the encoded format in which it was sent. As Internet e-mail software gets more and more sophisticated, this process of encoding and decoding often takes place automatically with no extra effort on the user's part. Currently, however, you may run into the problem of receiving files by e-mail that look like gibberish because of the lack of standardization among the various encoding schemes for e-mail attachments on the Internet.

Fortunately, programs are available that will translate from one encoding language into another. One such program which has gained popularity is called Wincode and is available as shareware on the Web at **http://www.furnation.com/tucows/comp.html#wincode**. If you belong to a commercial online service, you can locate this program using the Keyword search feature to locate Wincode.

If you need practice sending e-mail and attaching files, you can enlist the aid of a friend or simply send notes and attached files to yourself.

Zipping and Compressing Attached Files

Another technique for speeding the transmission of attached files is to compress or *zip* their contents into the smallest possible space. The smaller the file, the faster it will transmit from one computer to another. The most popular form of compression is called *zipping* and the files so compressed are called *zip* files. Commonly, many separate files can be zipped into a single archive. For example, if you wanted to send several chapters of a book via e-mail, you could create an archive called Book.zip (pronounced book dot zip) and add as many chapters as you desire in compressed format to this zipped archive. The beauty of zipping is that often the entire archive is no bigger than any of the individual unzipped files that it contains.

Zipping is done by special software that is available as shareware on the Internet. Two popular zipping programs are PKZip and Niko Mak Computing's WinZip which can be found at **http://www.winzip.com**.

E-Mail Commands

Once you compose or receive an e-mail message, you should be familiar with several command options on your e-mail software. Most of them have common sense names that are self-explanatory. The most popular commands include:

Send: After you are satisfied with what you have written, just click on Send to direct it onto the Internet. You must be connected online to use this option. Otherwise you can compose your message offline and choose the Send Later command to store your message until you next connect to the Internet.

Send Later: You can compose a message offline and save it until you go online again.

Reply: Clicking the Reply button gives you an e-mail template that is already addressed to the person who sent you the message. When replying to a message, it is useful to quote the part of the message to which you are responding.

Quote: Quoting means including a part (or all) of the original message so that the recipient knows what you are responding to. Quoting is usually done by blocking out a section of the original message and copying that block into the response. Anyone familiar with a word processor will have no difficulty marking a block of text.

Forward: Forwarding allows you to send a copy of the received message to another person. Some programs require you to block out the section of the original message that you wish to forward. If you just click on Forward, you may end up sending a blank page to the next recipient.

Delete: If you will never need to retrieve the message, just delete it from your hard disk.

Print: Clicking on Print sends the e-mail message to your printer. What else could it mean?

Store or Save: Most programs allow you to save messages to a directory on your hard disk. They can then be brought into a word processor for editing, for example.

E-Mail and the Myth of Privacy

E-mail gives the impression that it vanishes into cyberspace, never to be seen again. In reality, it is as traceable and identifiable as a written letter or a voice recording on a tape recorder. Mental health professionals need to be especially cognizant of maintaining confidentiality about patient information, especially if they are communicating by e-mail.

When you send e-mail into cyberspace, where does it go? The mail you send travels to the host computer used by its recipient where it is stored, pending its retrieval by the receiver's home computer. Even after the receiver downloads the message that you sent, a copy usually remains behind on the Internet service provider's computer or online service's (e.g., CompuServe) computer. Should you be involved in some kind of illegal activity, the government may be able to get a copy of your e-mail with a proper search warrant.

If you send e-mail on a local network at a school or job site, a copy of your message will most likely remain on the main computer and be accessible by the network administrator (who may be your boss). Should you be foolish enough to send sexually explicit, harassing, or offensive messages, chances are that the evidence of your misconduct will be readily available to the authorities.

Diane Schetksy, M.D. (1997), writing about the issues of privacy and electronic communications, cited Attorney Joan Feldman's five precautions, which she summarized as follows in the Winter 1997 issue of *Connecticut Psychiatrist*:

1. E-mails should be labeled as confidential information and instruction should be sent that they are not to be altered in any way.
2. Recognize that you lose control over anything you e-mail; recipients can disperse it as they choose.
3. Routinely delete the e-mail messages from your computer and make a printout of important ones.
4. Avoid offering opinions on cases through e-mail.
5. Exert particular care if using a shared/network computer system where there may be hundreds of copies of your e-mail. [p. 5]

Juno—a Free E-Mail Service

If your primary interest is e-mail service, you might want to consider Juno, an e-mail software package that you can use for free in most cities in the United States. Like radio and TV, Juno is supported by advertising. Quoted below are some excepts from Juno's page on the Web:

> Juno is a completely free Internet e-mail service. If you have a PC equipped with Microsoft Windows and a modem, you can use Juno to exchange e-mail with anyone in the world who has

> an Internet e-mail address, and never have to pay Juno anything. . . . When you use Juno, your computer communicates with Juno's central computers over your telephone line. They provide several hundred telephone numbers for their members to use and expect to offer even more in the future.

You can get more information about Juno on the WWW at **http://www.juno.com/** or by telephone at 1-800-654-JUNO for a copy of the software.

Bigfoot—Keep the Same E-mail Address Forever

Had I known about Bigfoot, I would not have suffered so much aggravation when Bill Gates summarily discontinued local MSN phone connections in my home state of Connecticut. Microsoft's arrogance forced me to switch to another server, which then necessitated notifying all my e-mail colleagues of the change of address. Bigfoot offers a free unchanging e-mail address on the Web. Once registered with Bigfoot, you can tell Bigfoot to forward your Bigfoot e-mail to any other address that you desire. You can change servers as often as you like and just notify Bigfoot of your new e-mail address to keep your electronic letters coming. You can find Bigfoot at **http://www.bigfoot.com/BFLife/bfl.htm**. I happen to like Bigfoot but several other sites also offer free e-mail and are listed in the directory section of this book.

MAILING LISTS, LISTSERV, MAJORDOMO, AND LISTPROC

As described in the previous chapter, mailing lists are discussion groups carried on by means of e-mail. There exist hundreds of mailing lists that cover just about every topic imaginable. Mailing lists may be managed either by a human who checks messages before passing them on (moderated lists) or automatically by a computer program that simply forwards all the messages it receives (unmoderated lists). Because it is so labor intensive, the management of most lists today is automated and the majority of mailing lists are unmoderated.

Mailing lists have two addresses, one for administrative purposes and another for posting the actual messages that comprise the list. If you wish to subscribe or cancel your subscription to a list, you write to the administrative or list-management address. If you wish to contribute comments to the list, you write to the posting address of the list.

A word of caution: joining a list can flood your e-mail box with an abundance of messages, and you will need to check your box almost daily. Think about this when you plan your next vacation. Some mailing lists offer *digests*, which are simply groups of messages sent as a single e-mail file. Many users find digests more convenient than receiving dozens of separate e-mail messages every week.

There are a couple dozen automated mailing list software programs that appear on the Net, with names like listserv, majordomo, listproc, mailserv, and almanac. The majority of unmoderated mailing lists are managed by listserv, majordomo, or listproc. To subscribe to a mailing list, you must obtain its administrative address and then send e-mail there requesting to join. If it's a listserv list, for example, you would send a subscription request to **listserv@ListAddress**.

To take a concrete example, suppose you were a college professor who wanted to participate in a discussion about the Holocaust. You might decide to subscribe to the Scholarly Holocaust Discussion List, a discussion group for college teachers interested in the Holocaust. The address of this list is **http://www.**

uicvm.uic.edu, and to subscribe you would send e-mail to **listserv@uicvm.uic.edu**. The body text of your e-mail should read: subscribe holocaus YourName (without the 't' in holocaust and YourName being your actual name).

Yet another example that illustrates the diversity of available mailing lists was sent to me in response to a message I had posted on the Internet asking for information about mailing lists related to psychology and mental health. The response read as follows:

> "PSYCH"—born September 21, 1995, 14:40 BST, London, England, for psychological astrology. To subscribe send E-mail to: *listserver@astrologer.com* with the message:
>
> *subscribe psych*
> *end*
>
> and you will receive all details. Moderator: Dermod Moore.

For more information about the three major mailing list software systems, you can send e-mail to the following addresses. Both the Subject heading and the body text of your e-mail should contain the single word "help." Here are the addresses:

listproc@inet.ed.gov
listserv@listserv.net
majordomo@greatcircle.com

Finally, to locate mailing lists that appeal to your interests you can check a couple of excellent sites on the Web. These include Publicly Accessible Mailing Lists compiled by Stephanie da Silva at **http://www.neosoft.com/internet/paml/** and RES-Links All-in-One Resource Page at **http://www.cam.org/~intsci/index.html**. Another resource is the file interest-groups.txt, which you can view or download via FTP at **ftp://nisc.sri.com/netinfo/**.

Mailing List Netiquette

Netiquette is a cute term for Internet etiquette. When posting to mailing lists, the proper lady or gentleman will refrain from flaming, spamming, and SHOUTING. It is also polite to speak only when you have something worthwhile to say. Why fill cyberspace with froth? You may want to lurk in the background, just reading other people's messages for a few days before you submit your first post. When responding to a message on the list, it helps other members if you quote a small segment of the original message to let everyone know where you are coming from and what you are talking about.

NEWSGROUPS

Newsgroups are discussion forums that are part of Usenet (the Users Network). *News* here refers to Usenet's topics of discussion rather than to traditional reporting that you might read in the newspaper or hear on the evening news. You can find a newsgroup about almost any topic imaginable, and estimates are that currently more than 15,000 newsgroups are in existence.

You gain access to newsgroups via your newsreader software, which is now a feature of the major World Wide Web browsers like Netscape and Microsoft Internet Explorer. Recall that unlike Web addresses, the newsgroup URL consists of the word "news" followed by a colon (:) followed by the name of the newsgroup. For example, if you were interested in finding a penpal, you could check out the newsgroup **soc.penpals** (pronounced "soc dot penpals") by entering the address **news:soc.penpals** into the URL slot of your Web browser.

Usenet organizes its groups into hierarchies of categories. The names of newsgroups consist of words separated by periods. These names begin with a general category's abbreviation, followed by a period or dot, followed by a more specific next level category. For example, the newsgroup **rec.games.video.nintendo** belongs to the general category Recreation and specifically discusses Nintendo video games.

Usenet started with seven broad categories (the original or traditional hierarchy) and eventually added several more (the alternative hierarchy). The original Usenet hierarchy consists of the following seven main topic areas:

comp: groups about computers
misc: miscellaneous topics
news: meaning news about Usenet newsgroups
rec: recreation, sports, hobbies, etc.
sci: science and research
soc: social, political, and cultural issues
talk: a place to express your opinions

Any topic that does not fit into the traditional seven falls into the alternative hierarchy. The names of alternative groups often begin with alt. These tend to be less formal and more free-wheeling than the traditional seven. Among alternative groups you can find frank discussions of sex (**alt.sex**) or such bizarre topics as the Fans of Newt Gingrich group (**alt.fan.newt-gingrich**). For newcomers (or *newbies*, as they are called on the Net), the alternatives hierarchy provides a welcoming committee, the **alt.newbie** group. Some other nontraditional groups are:

alt: alternative
bionet: about biology
bit: issues involving Bitnet "listserv" mailing lists
biz: about business

clari: ClariNet news service (which charges a fee!)
k12: for teachers K through 12
relcom: about the former USSR

Much of what we learned about mailing lists also applies to newsgroups, which consist of articles (messages of any length) about a particular topic. The major difference between newsgroups and mailing lists is that you read newsgroup articles via your newsreader software whereas mailing list messages are delivered directly to your e-mail address. Subscribers to newsgroups can read articles or messages that have been posted by others and may submit their own messages (posts) to the group. As usual, when you respond to an article, it is useful to quote the original message to which you are replying.

You can subscribe to newsgroups about topics that interest you, and your newsreader program will keep track of which articles you read. Newsgroups may be moderated by a human or may be unmoderated (managed automatically by a computer program). If you want to practice posting to a newsgroup, you can send a message to the **alt.test** group, whose computer will automatically let you know if you did a good job.

Newsgroups have a vocabulary of their own. Newsgroup articles are also called messages, posts, or postings. Simply reading all the posts without sending a message is called *lurking*. *Cross-posting* means posting the same message on several groups. Cross-posting is considered poor Netiquette because it clutters the Usenet with needless repetition and unnecessary traffic—it's like being a cyberspace road hog. A primary article and its ensuing discussion is called a *thread*. For example, a newsgroup about sexuality might contain threads about straight sex, gay sex, celibacy, and so on.

Most newsgroups have a file called the FAQ, meaning frequently asked questions. The FAQ gives the vital information about the group, its focus and intent, and its rules of Netiquette. As with mailing lists you should not SHOUT, spam (send junk mail), flame (act like a barbarian), or troll (try to provoke others to anger). Flaming can lead to a flame war—a thread of boorish, hostile, unmannered drivel—similar to a partisan debate in the United States Senate. I also suggest avoiding the use of too many emoticons in your posts.

5

TRADITIONAL TOOLS OF THE INTERNET: FTP, Archie, Gopher-Veronica-Jughead, Telnet, WAIS, Whois, Finger, and Ping

This chapter focuses on tools that were a traditional part of the Internet before the development of the World Wide Web, which is rapidly becoming the largest component of the Internet. Many of these tools are now incorporated into the modern Web browsers and function automatically in the background. Nonetheless, it is useful to know about these items because you will occasionally want to access Internet sites that are not part of the WWW and that require the use of one or more of these features. Even if you confine your use of the Internet to the World Wide Web, you will periodically come across the topics discussed below.

It may help to get an overview of the various resources on the Internet. The Internet is simply a giant network of all the computers in the world that are linked together electronically. Cyberspace is the name we use for all the information residing on the millions of computers that comprise the Internet. Because the information in cyberspace may be stored in different ways, cyberspace itself can be further subdivided according to the ways in which it makes information available. To use an analogy, cyberspace represents the entire universe of Internet resources, and the various Internet features are the galaxies that constitute that universe. The following list includes some of the most popular regions of cyberspace:

The World Wide Web, a huge network of Web pages connected by hypertext (http://) links.
E-mail, the electronic mail service.
Mailing lists.
Usenet newsgroups of discussions of many types.
Gopherspace consisting of Gopher "holes" that contain files and links to other resources easily accessed by plainly written Gopher menus.
FTP (file transfer protocol) sites where files are stored for transfer to and from other computers.
Archie sites containing a list of all the files available on FTP sites around the world.
IRC and other types of chat groups.
Telnet, a way to connect your computer to a host computer so that your PC acts like a dumb terminal that gives you access to that host.
WAIS, an old-fashioned wide area information server that does keyword searches of net-wide database indices.

For a discussion of Internet protocols and software tools, as well as a graphical map of cyberspace circa 1994, go to **http://eemgr.rmc.ca/module2.htm**.

DOWNLOADING AND UPLOADING: FILE TRANSFER PROTOCOL (FTP) AND ANONYMOUS FTP

Many universities, government agencies, corporations, and even individual computer users make files available at FTP sites as a public service. The file transfer protocol (FTP) is one of the most popular techniques on the Internet for transferring files from one computer to another. Using FTP, you can browse, upload, and download files on various computers around the world. It is possible to upload and download files without FTP, but that usually involves using the computer language UNIX with its not-so-obvious commands. I am assuming that most readers will not want to learn the UNIX language for sending or receiving files and would prefer instead to point and click with their mouse on a file name inside their Web browser or FTP software.

To download a file that resides on another computer, you must first gain access to that computer's files. Some host computers require you to log in and identify yourself by entering a password. Many host systems, however, give users free access to their files and do not require a password. Because the user remains anonymous to these free remote systems, they are called anonymous FTP sites. Anonymous FTP does not require you to establish an account with the host computer. Some hosts, however, do ask you to type the word *anonymous* as your log-in ID and to use your e-mail address (**YourName@ComputerDomain Name**) as your password.

FTP sites have names that often begin with the prefix ftp. For example, the FTP site of the Library of Congress is **ftp.loc.gov** and to get there you would enter the URL address **ftp://ftp.loc.gov/** into your Web browser's address slot. Having done so, you will see a root directory that lists the main directories at that site.

For example, **ftp.loc.gov** lists five main directories on its root directory, as follows:

FTP root at **ftp.loc.gov**

04/28/96 12:00AM Directory bin
09/05/96 12:00AM Directory etc
04/28/96 12:00AM Directory lib
03/12/97 12:15PM Directory pub
01/14/94 12:00AM Directory usr

Then, by clicking with your mouse on one of the items in the root directory, you will be able to see the contents of that directory. In this example, let's click on the Directory *pub* and see what happens. We are taken to the list of files in the directory *pub*:

FTP directory /pub/ at **ftp.loc.gov**

Up to higher level directory [Clicking on this line takes you back to the main directory]
10/19/94 12:00AM 144 .names
08/09/96 12:00AM 328,315 INDEX
12/07/94 12:00AM 5,899 README
09/05/96 12:00AM Directory about.internet
03/06/97 01:14PM Directory american.memory

And finally, clicking on the filename README we see the contents of that file, which begins as follows:

LIBRARY OF CONGRESS
FILES AVAILABLE THROUGH FTP
ftp.loc.gov (140.147.2.69)

> The Library of Congress has placed a variety of files on a central computer for anonymous file transfer by Internet users. The address of this FTP host is FTP.LOC.GOV (140.147.2.69). Once connected to this address, look in the /pub directory to find the various files and directories described below: . . .

This file goes on to describe the contents of all the FTP directories that are available at this site.

For a list of FTP sites on the World Wide Web, you can try the Monster FTP Sites List at **http://hoohoo.ncsa.uiuc.edu/ftp/** or the Washington University Data Archive at **http://wuarchive.wustl.edu/**. Lists of FTP sites usually specify whether the file is an IBM PC or a Macintosh format file because these two file types are incompatible. In addition, the FTP sites themselves normally store IBM PC and Macintosh files in separate directories. Most search engines on the Web allow you to search FTP sites. To assure access during peak traffic periods, many FTP sites maintain mirror sites that store the same files at several different computers on the Net.

File Names and File Types at FTP Sites

As mentioned previously, the files at the FTP sites reside in directories that are accessed via a root (main) directory for that site. You can think of the FTP host computer as a giant filing cabinet. Each item in the root directory is like one of the cabinet drawers, and within each drawer you may find file folders (subdirectories) and individual files. Windows 95 actually refers to the directories as *folders*.

In the example above we looked at the contents of the file at **ftp.loc.gov/pub/readme**. This name tells us that the file *readme* resides in the folder named *pub*, which is a directory at the FTP site **ftp.loc.gov**. Had we already known the name and address of this *readme* file, we could simply have entered **ftp://ftp.loc.gov/pub/readme** into the URL address slot of our Web browser to view the contents of the file.

Every file has a name that usually consists of two parts separated by a dot or period. The first part of the file name describes the contents of the file. The part after the dot, the *file extension*, identifies the type of file. Files ending in *.txt* are ASCII text files that contain only standard keyboard characters and can be read by any computer. The remainder are binary files that contain material other than ASCII text and must be accessed by a particular type of computer or software program. Some common file extensions are:

.arc	IBM PC compressed file
.arj	IBM PC compressed file
.au	audio or sound file
.avi	audiovisual file
.bat	a batch file
.bin	MacBinary file for Macintosh
.bmp	a graphics (picture) file
.com	executable or program (command) file
.doc	document or word processing file
.exe	executable or program file
.gif	a type of graphics file
.htm	hypertext markup language WWW file (DOS/Windows)
.html	hypertext markup language file, a text file used on the WWW (UNIX)
.jpg	a type of compressed graphics file
.lzh	IBM PC compressed file
.mov	video (movie) file

.mpg	compressed video file
.pict	Macintosh graphics or picture file
.sea	Macintosh self-extracting archive file
.sit	Macintosh Stuffit compressed archive
.txt	non-binary (plain keyboard) text or ASCII file
.wav	audio or sound (wave) file
.uu or .uue	UNIX UUencoded
.zip	a compressed or IBM PC PKZIP file that needs to be unzipped
.zoo	compressed archive file

WS_FTP.EXE—A Useful FTP Shareware Program

The shareware program **WS_FTP.EXE** allows you to transfer several files at a time and can be a real timesaver if you do a lot of uploading or downloading at FTP sites. When you use this program, you will see a list of the files on your own computer on the left side of the screen, and on the right side you will see a listing of the files on the remote system. You can use your mouse or the Shift or Control keys to select multiple files and transfer them with the arrow keys between the two computers. You can get a copy of **WS_FTP.EXE** at any of the following URL addresses:

http://www.wt.net/WT.net/ws_ftp1.htm#WS_FTP
http://www.ccm.net/ftp-web.html
http://www.technopolis.or.th/w_tcpip/ws_ftp.htm
http://www.mcs.anderson.edu/personalpages/ws_ftp.html
ftp://ftp.cica.indiana.edu

THE ARCHIE FTP SEARCH TOOL

Suppose you know the name of a file but you don't know which FTP site houses it. Archie, an Internet tool named after the comic book character Archie, can come to the rescue. An Archie site is simply a location on an Internet computer that maintains a database or index of all the available FTP files in the world. To search an Archie site, you must know the name of the file you are seeking. If you are doing a general search and don't know the file's name, Archie will be of little assistance. The World Wide Web and its modern search engines are rapidly rendering Archie obsolete. For more about Archie and links to Archie servers, go to **http://archie.luth.se/searching.html** or **http://cuisun9.unige.ch/archie.html**.

GOPHER—THE INTERNET RODENT—AND HIS FRIENDS, VERONICA AND JUGHEAD

The Golden Gopher is the mascot of the University of Minnesota. Gophers are burrowing or tunneling American rodents with large cheek pouches. An office gopher is someone whose job is to "go for" things. When the folks at the University of Minnesota developed a way to burrow though cyberspace in search of information, they named their electronic rodent "Gopher" after the school mascot. Once the Gopher locates the material you are seeking, it presents you with a menu in ordinary language of links to the information you desire. Because Gophers are mainly text-based, they are much faster to access than the graphics-intensive World Wide Web. According to current estimates, there are about eight thousand Gopher-infested computers worldwide. Internet aficionados refer to Gopher sites as "Gopher holes" and call the part of cyberspace where the Gophers reside "Gopherspace."

The information available via Gopher is often ASCII text, but binary files are also included at Gopher sites. To access the information, you simply click on the menu item and you are taken to the file or resource that you are looking for. If you click on a file name, that file will download to your computer and be displayed on your monitor. If you click on a link to another resource, you will travel to the next computer, which may be another Gopher site but may also be another Internet resource such as an FTP site, a Usenet newsgroup, an Archie server, and so on. Like FTP sites, each Gopher hole can only allow a limited number of participants at any given time. If you can't gain access, you will have to try again later.

The place to start your exploration of Gopherspace is none other than the University of Minnesota's Gopher site **gopher.tc.umn.edu**, which offers a listing of all the Gopher sites in the world. To get there, you simply type **gopher://gopher.tc.umn.edu/** into your Web browser's URL/address/locator box and press Enter. You will then arrive at a page entitled Gopher root at **gopher.tc.umn.edu**, where you will see the root Gopher menu. The root menu is a main menu that offers a broad list of options. Selecting an item on the main menu will take you to a submenu that has more specificity. You can travel up and down menus looking for the information you have in mind. Another useful starting point is the Gopher directory at Rice University, whose URL is **gopher://riceinfo.rice.edu/11/Subject** and whose root directory is called Gopher directory at **riceinfo.rice.edu**.

Some users regard Gopher as the ancient history of the Internet, and in fact most information on the Net is now available on the World Wide Web. It may happen, however, that a particular file or bit of data that you want has not yet been converted to a Web page and may only be available through your electronic rodent. For more information about Gopher and useful links to

Gopher sites, go to **http://www.nvds.com/gopher.html** or **http://www.izzy.net/newgophe.htm**.

Veronica and Jughead

Veronica is the Gopher's Gopher. It was developed at the University of Nevada and is a catalogue of all the Gopher menus in the world. If you don't know which particular Gopher site to search, you can ask Veronica for help. The name Veronica is an acronym for Very Easy Rodent Oriented Net-wide Index of Computerized Archives. Recall that Gopher creates an index of the information at Gopher sites and presents you with plain language menus of what is available.

Veronica goes a step further and creates an index of all the Gopher menu titles in the world. At regular intervals, Veronica burrows to every Gopher site on the Net and updates her listing of all Gopher menu items available. A keyword search of Veronica will tell you which Gopher holes hold your pot of gold. Because Veronica must search the entirety of Gopherspace, she is not the fastest lady in the world. For readers who are fond of the Miller analogies, Veronica is to Gopher as Archie is to FTP.

Jughead, which stands for Jonzy's Universal Gopher Hierarchy Excavation and Display, is a deluxe variant of Veronica. Like Veronica, Jughead maintains an index of all Gopher menus in the world. Jughead has the advantage, however, of allowing you to confine your search to a small area of Gopherspace. Because it does a more limited search, Jughead is usually speedier than Veronica, who is out searching the globe. For more information about Veronica and Jughead, look at **http://www.uia.ac.be/ext/gopher.html**, or **http://www.agrenv.mcgill.ca/SEARCH/GOSEARCH.HTM**, or **http://opim.wharton.upenn.edu/~serdar93/internet/veronica.html**.

TELNET

Telnet is a computer program that allows your personal computer to act like a dumb terminal of the host computer to which it is connected via the Internet. To establish a Telnet connection, you usually need to enter a login ID and a password. Many Telnet connections are free and require the use of a user ID such as "guest" or "new user." A message on the screen often instructs you which login ID and password to enter.

Once you have connected via Telnet to a host computer, you can often run programs and access data on that host. Many online games require Telnet connections, and some libraries require Telnet to gain access to their computerized card catalogues. For practice you might want to check out the library site Biblioteca Mid-York Library System by typing **telnet://libvax1.midyork.lib.ny.us/** into the URL/address/locator box on your Web browser and pressing Enter. This site came in handy when my 13-year-old son had to look up some references for the bibliography of his assigned term paper on Japanese fashion, a topic dear to the heart of an adolescent male. For more information about Telnet, go to **http://www.ldeo.columbia.edu/unixhelp/networks_ telnet.html** or **http://www.webdzine.com/tutorials/telnet.html**.

WAIS

WAIS of the Internet is not a psychological test. Instead, WAIS stands for Wide Area Information Service, a method used to search for information using keywords expressed in plain language. When you do a WAIS search, you are presented with a list of documents ranked according to how frequently they meet the search criteria. Many Web Search Engines are based on

WAIS technology. Further information about WAIS can be found at **http://salve2.salve.edu/inter-query.html** or **http://www.fedworld.gov/wais.htm**.

WHOIS, FINGER, AND PING (INTERNET SONAR)

This final assortment of Internet tools is worth mentioning, at least in passing. You never know when one of them might come in handy.

Whois is a little Internet program that does what its name implies. If you give a host computer's domain name to the Whois program, it will return the vital statistics of the company related to the computer with that name. Specifically, Whois can tell you the name, address, phone number, and e-mail address of the company that owns a particular host computer.

Finger is a command from the UNIX computer language that displays information about a particular user on the Internet. The Finger program can show who is currently connected to a computer and might tell you their real name, the time they logged on, whether they have unread e-mail, how many other people are logged on, and so on. The annals of Internet history tell the story of a group of students at Carnegie Mellon who discovered that the local Coke machine was connected to the distributor via the Internet. These enterprising students Fingered the machine so they wouldn't have to walk all the way from their dorm rooms to the canteen and discover it was empty. More commonly, at a UNIX prompt you would type "finger" followed by a name to get a list of all the people with that name who have accounts on the computer you are using.

Ping is a little Internet tool that can check connections on the Net by sending a brief series of message packets to a remote computer with instructions to return the messages immediately.

Ping acts like a submarine's sonar ping, or like the return of a ping-pong ball. By timing the round trip of these data packets, Ping can tell you if the other computer is functional and how heavy the traffic is on the Net. Ping can also send back information on the routes traveled by its data packets and identify hang-ups or dysfunctional nodes on the Net.

For more information about Whois, Finger, and Ping, check out **http://sparc.tryc.on.ca/util.phtml** or **http://www.sharepaper.com/apps/reviews/cyberkit.html**. Those who read Spanish will find an excellent discussion of all the Internet tools in this chapter on the Web page entitled Internet Y Sus Herramientas Basicas at **http://jarthe.com/rim/docs/internet.htm**.

6 THE WORLD WIDE WEB

Because of its vivid graphics and easy accessibility, the World Wide Web has become the most popular frontier of cyberspace. Prior to the birth of the Web, Internet junkies had to content themselves with text-based forages through Gopherspace, Usenet newsgroups, FTP sites, e-mail, and so on. Web servers (host computers that house Web sites) made their first public appearance on the Internet early in 1993 and rapidly became the dominant force in cyberland. The rest is history, and now millions of users are surfing the Web.

The World Wide Web as we know it today originated at CERN, the European Particle Physics Laboratory in Switzerland. Its inventor, Tim Berners-Lee, designed a method for researchers to link pages of information by using *hypertext* technology. Simply by clicking on a keyword (link) in one document, the reader could go (surf) to a related document, which in turn contained its own links to other related documents.

Web pages are written in a special language called hypertext markup language (HTML). They have filenames that end with the extension .htm or .html to indicate that they are hypertext documents. Hypertext markup language allows the writer to create links to other Internet resources from within the text. These links usually appear as highlighted or underlined words on the Web page, but links may also be graphic images. The computer's mouse frequently changes from an arrow to a little hand with finger pointing when it alights upon a hypertext link, and clicking with the mouse on a hypertext link takes you to the related document.

Access to Web documents occurs via software called a Web browser, examples of which include Mosaic, Netscape Navigator, and Microsoft Internet Explorer. When your browser connects with a Web page, the host computer sends the contents of the HTML document to your computer using a technique called the hypertext transfer protocol (HTTP). As you recall, the web uses uniform resource locators (URLs) to identify sites on the Internet. To tell your browser which Web site to contact, you begin the Web address by indicating the HTTP protocol with "http://" followed by the Web page's domain, directory, and file names. In addition, other Internet tools such as FTP, Gopher, WAIS, e-mail, and Telnet are embedded in the Web hypertext links, which makes it possible to use these older Internet utilities directly from your Web browser. The following list summarizes the URL conventions for the beginning of various types of addresses in your Web browser:

FTP site: *ftp://site-name*
Gopher site: *gopher://site-name*
Telnet site: *telnet://site-name*
Web page: *http://site-name*

The very first Web interface was the *line mode browser*, which was soon replaced by Lynx, a text-based, nongraphical Web browser that offered both a menu and hypertext links. Lynx was developed at the University of Kansas and offered direct connections to Web, Gopher, and FTP sites. Although Lynx is a powerful and fast Web browser, it offers only menus and text and was soon supplanted by Mosaic, a graphical Web browser.

GRAPHICAL WEB BROWSERS

NCSA Mosaic was the first graphical web browser. It was quickly followed by Netscape Navigator (at **http://www.netscape.com/comprod/mirror/index.html**), the current leader in the field, and by Microsoft Internet Explorer (at **http://www.microsoft.com/ie/ie.htm**), Netscape's chief competi-

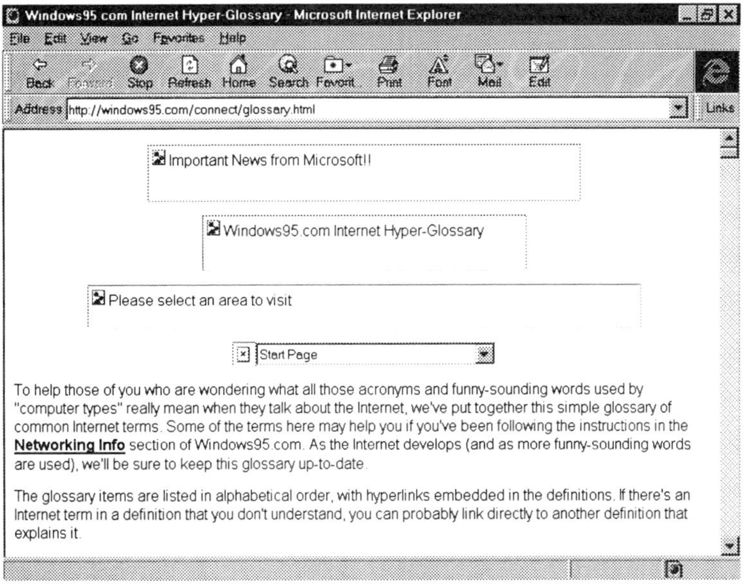

tor, both of which you can download for free from the Internet. In addition, the commercial online services like America Online offer their own Web browsers, which look and feel much like the Netscape and Microsoft browsers. The advantage of so much similarity among the major Web browsers is that the user can easily transfer knowledge of one brand of browser software to another. The image on page 79 is a Print Screen image of the Microsoft Internet Explorer.

In the above example, we have used Microsoft Internet Explorer to go to a Web page entitled Windows95.com Internet Hyper-Glossary," at the URL listed in the address window. To increase the speed of transfer, I had set the browser to turn off the graphics. In the place of what would display as pictures, there appear instead little boxes. In the body of the text you will see

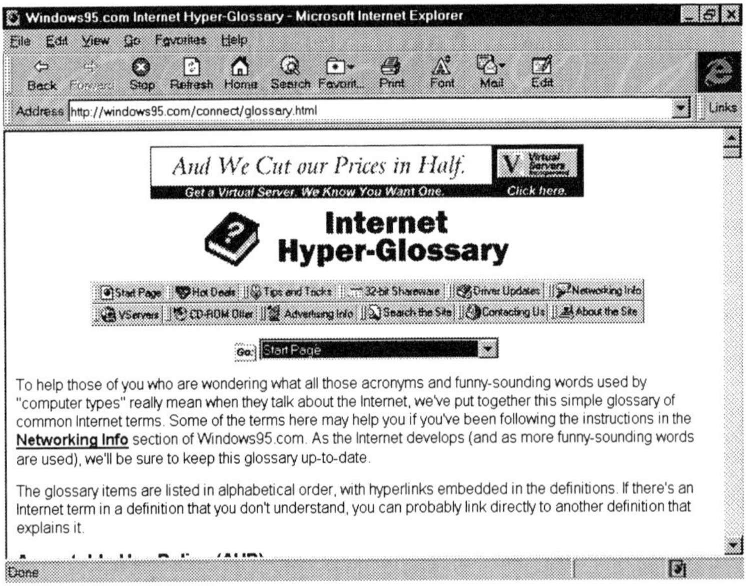

the underlined hypertext link Networking Info. Clicking on that link would take you to the Web page with that name. Once you use a link, its text changes to a different color. Hence, when you return to this page, you will know that you have already followed that particular link into cyberspace. Color changing links are a great help in navigating pages that contain multiple links to other Web sites.

In case you are wondering, the same page viewed with graphics turned on is on page 80.

Common Features of Web Browsers

The different varieties of Web browsing software all have certain features in common. Using the Microsoft Internet Explorer (see image above) as an example, I will list and describe what you can expect to find in a typical browser. These include:

Location/Address/URL box or window: This is a space where you can enter the URL (uniform resource locator) address of the Web page you want to view. Many browsers also allow you to enter the URL addresses of newsgroups and of Gopher and FTP sites, making special software for these applications obsolete.

History List: Browsers keep track of the addresses of all the Web pages that you visit during any given session. You can gain access to the history list by clicking on a little box containing an arrow at the right-hand side of the Location/Address/URL window. By clicking on any address in the history list, you can quickly view the page at that address.

Back: When you click on the Back button, you will go back to the page you most recently visited.

Forward: This is the button you click when you have gone back to previously visited sites and wish to move forward in your history list, one page at a time.

Refresh or Reload: Clicking on Refresh instructs the browser to reach out to the host computer in cyberspace and reload the page that you are currently viewing. Refreshing pages is useful when you are viewing Web pages that are updated frequently. Most Web browsers store a copy of the pages you have recently viewed in a special directory called a *cache* on the user's hard disk. Keeping a copy of Web pages on your computer's hard disk eliminates the need to read from the host computer each time you wish to view a Web site. Caches greatly speed up Web surfing because reading a file from your own hard disk is much faster than reading via modem. The problem is that when files change on the host computer, the Web browser will continue to read a previously visited site from your own cache unless you instruct it to refresh the Web page to obtain the most recent copy. Most browsers allow you to empty your cache, and it is a good idea to do so periodically. For example, in Microsoft Internet Explorer, under View, you would click on Options, Advanced, Settings, and Empty Folder to remove temporary Internet files.

Home, Home on the Web: Home is where the heart is. Clicking on Home tells the browser to go to the page you consider home base on the Web. Browsers come preset with a home page, but they give you the option of selecting which page will be the first to be displayed when you start your browser. Many users design their own personal home page and set it as their browser's place to begin surfing the Net. We will look at creating a personal Web page at the end of this chapter.

Bookmarks/Hot Lists/Favorite Places: It is not easy to remember the addresses of all the pages you visit. To help you return to the places you like, browsers allow you to tag Web pages that you want to visit again. These tags are called variously *bookmarks, hotlists*, or *favorite places*. By clicking on the Bookmark button, you can see a list of the names and addresses of your favorite sites. When you select one of these sites with your mouse, the browser displays that page on your screen.

Stop: Clicking on Stop instructs your browser to stop loading the page at the address in the URL box from the host computer. This can be helpful when there is a lot of traffic on the net and the browser seems to get stuck or to take forever to display the Web page. Or if you don't like what is beginning to appear on your screen, you may want to stop and surf elsewhere instead of waiting for the entire Web page to download.

Mail or E-Mail: Many browsers have a button that takes you to its e-mail features, eliminating the need for separate e-mail software.

News: Your browser may have a separate News command that calls forth the software needed for retrieving and posting to Usenet newsgroups.

Print: As the name implies, clicking the Print button sends the contents of the Web page to your printer, should you desire a hard copy.

Options or Preferences: Most browsers have an Options button that lets you set your preferences for certain features. On the Microsoft browser, the Options button is a choice on the menu listed under View. One useful option is the ability to turn graphics (pictures) on and off. Graphics look attractive but when Net traffic is heavy, they can take cyber-eons to transfer to your computer. If you are seeking text-based information, turning off the graphics can make your browser navigate the Web with the speed of lightning. If you come across a page whose graphics you wish to view, you can turn the graphics back on and then click Refresh to see the graphic presentation.

Source or HTML Code: Browsers allow you to view the HTML language code for the page you are viewing, a useful feature if you are trying to learn HTML to edit your own home page and want to see how others use the language. This item can be found under View in the Microsoft browser.

Exit: There are two ways to exit from your browser. One is to click the mouse on the letter X in the upper right hand corner. The other is to click on the File menu and then click on Exit. Quitting your browser may leave you still connected to your Internet provider, especially if you have other Internet software running. Most providers offer a simple command or menu item for disconnecting your phone line from the provider. If you have a commercial service like CompuServe or AOL, you can exit the Web browser and remain connected to the other features of the online service.

SEARCH ENGINES ONLINE

The Web contains millions of pages. How do you know where to start? Perhaps the most sensible place is at one of the Web directories or one of the Web search engines on the Net. A search engine is simply a software program that maintains an index of Web pages and searches for topics of your choosing in cyberspace. Most search engines are free and have their own addresses on the Web. You simply enter the URL of the search engine in the Locator/Address/URL box and press Enter. The directory section of this text contains a list of many of the available search engines, and new ones seem to sprout up frequently on the Net.

Some users select their favorite search engine as their browser's home page, or else put a link to their favorite search engine on their personal home page. Another option is to select as the home page of your browser a site offering links to topics of interest. For example, readers interested in mental health might begin browsing at Mental Health Net at **http://www.cmhc.com/**—"the largest, most comprehensive guide to mental health online, featuring over 6,000 individual resources."

How do Web directories and search engines know what is available on the Web and on the Net? There are two methods for search engines to become aware of pages on the Web. Authors of Web pages can directly submit their URL for inclusion in a search engine. Secondly, the search tools themselves send out programs called spiders, crawlers, worms, or robots to travel from page to page through Webspace, following the hypertext links and sending information on each site back to the main search engine program, which then creates or updates its index. Some of these robots travel through Usenet newsgroups, FTP sites, and other non-Web regions of cyberspace. Because Web pages come and go so rapidly on the Net, these worms and spiders must constantly roam through Webspace in search of its ever-changing information, and no search engine can ever be completely up-to-date.

Like moderated and unmoderated newsgroups, search engines come in two principal varieties: human mediated and computer automated. Each search engine maintains an index of all the Web pages that it selects for inclusion into its database. The various search engines on the Net have different inclusion criteria and will produce different results. Consequently, you may need to use several search engines to find the desired information.

Yahoo (**http://www.yahoo.com/**) and Webcrawler (**http://www.webcrawler.com/**) rely on human intervention. Yahoo, often referred to as a Web directory, is like the subject catalogue in a library because it classifies all the Web pages in its database into categories selected by its human managers. Such a system has an advantage for human users who categorize information into similar topics and subtopics. Yahoo allows you to search for Web sites, e-mail addresses, and Usenet newsgroups, and provides links to many useful information sites containing news, weather, maps, phone directories, and so on. Typical Yahoo categories include items such as these (quoted from **http://events.yahoo.com/**):

Arts and Entertainment
Business and Economy
Computers and Internet
Government
News and Media
Recreation
Regional
Science
Society and Culture
Sports

With so many interesting categories to choose from, what do people actually search for on Yahoo? A Web page entitled Callahan Online (**http://eyescream.com/yahootop200.html**) catalogues each month's two hundred most commonly entered keywords for a Yahoo search. In March of 1997, the top ten Yahoo search words were, in order: sex, chat, XXX, Playboy, Netscape software, nude, porno, games, porn, and weather. Items 11 through 20 included more sexually oriented terms plus maps, Halloween, and music. Items 21 through 30 added, in order: erotica, Microsoft, jokes, shareware, magazines, pictures, employment, jobs, erotic, and gay. To summarize Callahan's data, it appears that most Yahoo users are looking for sexually oriented and pornographic sites, chats, software, Netscape and Microsoft downloads and support, games, weather reports, maps, music, Halloween, magazines, jobs, and gay sites. Since one can enter several words into a Yahoo search, it may be that the most popular search phrase was "sex chat XXX." No wonder the conservatives in Congress are so upset.

The alternative to the human Web directory system offered by Yahoo is a search engine that simply classifies Web sites by keywords and does not put them into subject categories. AltaVista is such a prototypical keyword search engine with several nice features. It is a large database that catalogues both the Web and Usenet newsgroups. Amazingly, AltaVista indexes every word on a Web page and then permits searches by keywords and key phrases. AltaVista presents its search results with relevance rankings (how many of your search terms appear on the Web page) as well as the first several lines of text on the Web page.

Another useful feature of AltaVista is its ability to do Boolean searches using Boolean operations like OR, AND, NOT, or NEAR. For example, if you were interested in dreams and psychotherapy, you could do the following types of searches:

dreams AND psychotherapy—to find pages containing both keywords;

dreams OR psychotherapy—to find pages containing either keyword;

dreams NOT psychotherapy—to find pages about dreams but not psychotherapy;

dreams NEAR psychotherapy—to find pages containing the word "dream" in close proximity to the word "psychotherapy" (you can specify how close)—useful if you know two or more keywords in a title but not the exact title.

Another search engine with excellent Boolean search capabilities is Open Text Index at **http://www.opentext.com**.

For further information online, you can read the discussion in Spidap's Basic Search Engine FAQ ("How to get the most from search engines like AltaVista, Infoseek, Excite, Webcrawler, Lycos, HotBot, Open Text and the Yahoo Directory") at **http://www.monash.com/spidap2.html**.

SEARCH ENHANCEMENTS AND OFFLINE BROWSERS

Several commercial programs are available to help organize your searches and manage the results. Web Buddy is a typical example of such a search engine assistant. According to its advertising (**http://www.dataviz.com/webbuddy8**), Web Buddy helps you to "collect, convert, reuse and organize all the info you find on the Internet." You can save Web pages or whole Web sites to your hard disk and browse them offline as time permits, or if you wish you can convert Web pages and graphics to a form that can be read by your word processor or graphics program. Many of these programs allow you to schedule searches and download Web pages automatically, even when you are not at the computer. Some of the search enhancement programs (like Smart Bookmarks) check whether your favorite sites have changed their URLs on the Web and then update your bookmarks with the new addresses. Because new commercial enhancements are constantly appearing, I would advise readers to check reviews in a computer magazine or browse their favorite computer store's shelves before making a purchase.

URL-MINDER

URL-Minder is an online service that monitors Web pages of your choice and notifies you by e-mail when they change. The URL-Minder service is free, and you can register at **http://www.netmind.com/URL-minder/new/register.html**. I use URL-Minder to remind me whenever new virus definitions are available for the Norton AntiVirus program that is installed on my computer. The address of the Virus Update page is **http://www.hitchhikers.net/antivirus/antivirus-dis.phtml?thisone=NAV-Win**.

PLUG-INS

No matter how powerful the modern graphical Web browsers appear to be, somebody always thinks of something they are lacking and develops a companion program called a *plug-in* to enhance the browser's capabilities. Popular plug-ins include such programs as Acrobat Amber Reader, which enables you to view .pdf or portable document format graphical images; RealAudio, which allows you to listen to worldwide radio broadcasts over the Internet; QuickTime, Apple's video format for .mov movie files; and ShockWave, a multimedia utility at **http://www.macromedia.com/**.

There is an extensive list of plug-ins on the Web at Browser Watch Plug-In Plaza, **http://browserwatch.iworld.com/plugin.html**. For Netscape Navigator plug-ins, try Netscape's Home Page at **http://www.netscape.com/**, and for Microsoft Internet

Explorer plug-ins, go to Microsoft's page at **http://www. microsoft. com/**. You can also find a useful tutorial on plug-ins and other Internet features at **http://training.cit.cornell.edu/courses/ BeyondBrowsing/WebRes.html**. Michele Hoffman, author of the section on plug-ins, begins her page with the following:

> As good as the newest version of Netscape Navigator may be, not even the best Web browser gives you instant access to all of the interactivity and multimedia wonders of the Web. Pop in a plug-in, though, and you take browsing to another level. Browser add-ons, or plug-ins as they're commonly called, allow you to run animation, video, and audio programs all within your browser—without ever having to open a separate helper application. Once they've been downloaded and installed, plug-ins work seamlessly within your browser by simply firing themselves up as needed. The catch?

Sorry, you'll have to read the rest of her page at **http:// zuni.cnet.com/Content/Features/Techno/Plugins/** to find out the catch.

JAVA

Java is a programming language developed by Sun Microsystems. Small programs called Applets can be written in Java and then embedded in Web pages. When your Web browser comes upon a Java Applet, it can run the Java program on the remote computer without that program having to reside on your hard drive. Java Applets provide many of the bells and whistles of modern graphical Web sites. For more information, consult the Java Links page at **http://sunsite.unc.edu/javafaq/links. html**, or go to the page entitled Welcome to Presenting Java at **http://www.december.com/works/java.html**, which begins with the words:

Java™ is a computer programming language that brings animation and a level of interactivity to the Web that has never been possible before. With Java, you can create animations, simulations, and applications for Web pages that are truly interactive.

SECURITY ON THE WEB: IS BIG BROTHER WATCHING?

Because confidential information travels across the Web, various schemes have been developed for providing security and encrypting information. Encryption involves the coding of information prior to transmission. Encrypted files must be decoded (decrypted) by the recipient. Popular methods of encryption include Pretty Good Privacy (PGP) for e-mail, Rotate 13 (ROT 13) for newsgroups, Secure HyperText Transfer Protocol (SHTTP) for the Web, and Secure Sockets Layer (SSL) for the Net and the Web.

The United States government is opposed to Pretty Good Privacy-encrypted e-mail because it is so hard to crack. Instead, Uncle Sam would prefer the Clipper Chip method of encryption because it would allow only the government to be able to decode secure information on the Internet. Needless to say, the Clipper Chip has caused quite a stir on the Net, where it is referred to the Big Brother Chip or the Wiretap Chip. For more insight into this cyberspace controversy, read "The Clipper Chip versus The CypherPunks" at **http://shakti.trincoll.edu/~ssalsbur/clipper/clipper.html** or the Cypherpunks Home Page at **http://www.ilf.net/crypto/**.

Finally, for more than you ever wanted to know about security on the Net, read the FAQ at **http://www-genome.wi.mit.edu/WWW/faqs/www-security-faq.html** or to **http://perl.guru.org/faqs/www-security-faq.html**, where you will find a detailed technical discussion.

PARENTAL GUIDANCE: SECURITY AT HOME

Because children using the Net can access the same sites that are available to adults, many parents are concerned about easy access to pornographic and other objectionable material. The same child who is banned from entering an adult book store can freely download XXX material from the Internet. Of even more concern is the possibility of children being seduced by unscrupulous characters or cult leaders whom they may meet in chat groups. A slew of companies have written software programs that allow parents to block objectionable material from being accessed and displayed by your Web browser. You will find several of them listed alphabetically under Parental Guidance in the directory section of this text.

CREATING YOUR OWN HOME PAGE

Part of the fun of the World Wide Web is the opportunity it offers to express your creativity by designing and publishing your own home page on the Web. As hypertext editing software becomes more sophisticated and user-friendly, it is becoming easier to create an attractive Web site of your very own. For a list of Web sites where you can obtain software and tutorials on creating Web pages, see the section entitled HTML: Hyptertext Markup Language Editors in the directory section of this text. We will end this chapter with a very brief lesson on HTML.

If all you want is only a plain vanilla, text-based presence on the Web, try **http://www.inc.com/createsite/**. If you want to get fancier and/or add graphics to your Web page, you will need an add-in for your word processor, or else a dedicated Web page editor like HotDog or Web-It! 32. All of these programs can be downloaded from the Net.

Some services on the Web offer easy Web page editors. You just fill in the blanks and the editor designs the page for you. My favorite of these is Angelfire at **http://www.angelfire.com/**. See the entries under Home Pages in the directory section of this text for other sites. Finally, readers who subscribe to America Online should be aware that AOL provides its members with 10 MB of space to store files that can be part of a Web site. AOL also makes available a simple Web page editor for its members.

HTML BASICS FOR THE ADVENTUROUS BEGINNER

You will probably need to know something about hypertext markup language (HTML) to design your own Web site. Whole books have been written about HTML, and if you get interested you will need to read one of them. In this section we will attempt only the briefest introduction. In essence, HTML is a way of tagging or coding text with certain commands that are contained in brackets of the form < > to tell the Web browser how to display your text, graphics, or other features of your Web page.

Many HTML tags come in pairs that tell the browser when to begin displaying a certain feature and when to stop. For example, < i > some words < /i > would display the "some words" in the center in italics as *some words*. The backslash (/) within the brackets is an HTML convention for stopping or turning off the code. Here is a list of some of the more common HTML paired codes and their meanings:

<html> </html>	The page between these tags is an HTML document.
<head> </head>	Text between these tags constitutes the page's header.
<title> </title>	This defines a space for the page's title.

<body> </body>	The body text of your page goes between these tags.
<b> </b>	Text between these tags appears in **bold**.
<i> </i>	Text between these tags appears in *italics*.
<ol> </ol>	The text between these tags forms an ordered or numbered list.
<ul> </ul>	The text between these tags forms an unnumbered list.

Other important, but non-paired HTML codes, include:

 	Places a line break after a sentence or piece of text.
<hr>	This draws a horizontal line (rule) across the page.
<li>	The text following <li> is part of a list.
<p>	Creates a line break and puts an empty line after it.

A combination of paired and nonpaired HTML codes is used to identify links to other Web sites, using the following code:

<a href = "URL"> *link-name* </a>

For example, <a href = "**http://www.aronson.com**"> *Jason Aronson Inc.* </a>
 would appear on a Web page as an underlined hypertext link as follows:

Jason Aronson Inc.

If you were to click with your mouse on *Jason Aronson Inc.*, your browser would go to **http://www.aronson.com**.

Let me conclude this chapter with a sample HTML Web page, my own home page on AOL.

EXAMPLE WEB SITE: THE AUTHOR'S HOME PAGE IN HTML

The following is the HTML code for my Web page on AOL at **http://members.aol.com/tonylouis/home/dsm.htm**. It will change from time to time as I revise and update my Web site.

```
<html>

<header>
<title>Psychiatric Diagnosis and Transcultural Psychiatry</
   title>
</header>

<body bgcolor="#e7c4af" background="/bg/firering.jpg"
text="#000000" link="#000000" vlink="#2400ff">

<!--Header-->
<h1 align=center>Psychiatric Diagnosis</h1>
<h2 align=center> and Transcultural Psychiatry</h2>
<h3 align=center>A Home Page of Anthony L. LaBruzza and
   José M. Méndez-Villarrubia</h3>
<!--EndHeader-->

<basefont size=4>
<center><img src="http://members.aol.com/tonylouis/
   home/dsm.gif" align=middle></center>
<p>

<!--List-->
```

```
<font size=+2>Topics of Interest:</font>
<ul>
<li>DSM-IV and ICD-10
<li>Transcultural Psychiatry and Psychology
<li>Ataques de Nervios
<li>Assessment of Hispanic (Latino) Clients
<li>Spanish Language and Culture
<li>Community Mental Health
<li>Dialectical Behavior Therapy (DBT) for Latino Clients
</ul>
<p>
<!--EndList-->

<!--Links-->
<font size=+2>Favorite Links</font><p>
<a href="http://www.cmhc.com">Mental Health Net
   links to thousands of sites</a><br>
<a href="http://www.demon.net/inews/search.html">
   Demon Internet Search Page</a><br>
<a href="http://www2.gc.net/rwclements/"> Ray's
   Windows 95 Support, Upgrades, etc.</a><br>
<a href="http://www.geocities.com/Athens/Acropolis/
   7409/"> WebSpañol Spanish Language Site</a><br>
<a href="http://www.datatrackinc.com"> DataTrack
   Home Page Developer</a><br>
<a href="http://www.ciudadfutura.com/cgi-localbin/
   horoscopo/tao.pl"> Daily Quote en español from the
   Tao Te Ching by Lao Tsu</a><br>
<a href="http://www.intercom.es/navegador/busca.
   htm"> Buscadores y Mapas</a><br>
<a href="http://www.angelfire.com"> Angelfire - Easiest
   Free Home Pages</a><br>
```

```
<a href="http://www.angelfire.com/az/nazaire/index.
   html"> Hertz Nazaire's Sickle Cell Anemia Page Ser-
   vices</a><br>
<p>
<!--EndLinks-->
<p>

<!--Freetext-->
<p>
This page is dedicated to psychiatric assessment and
   diagnosis and to issues in transcultural psychiatry,
   especially the assessment of Hispanic clients in the
   United States.<p>We have written a book entitled
   <B><I>Using DSM-IV: A Clinician's Guide to Psychiatric
   Diagnosis </I></B>, (1996, Jason Aronson Inc.) in
   which we discuss these issues. For further information
   or to order books online at a <I><B> 20% discount</
   B></I> go to <a href="http://www.aronson.com">
   The Jason Aronson Inc. Home Page</a><br> <p>We are
   currently working with several colleagues at the
   Greater Bridgeport Community Mental Health Center
   to translate Marsha Linehan's manual on Dialectical
   Behavioral Therapy into Spanish for use with Latino
   populations.
<!--EndFreetext-->
<p>

<!--Email-->
<center>Email to Anthony LaBruzza at:<a
href="mailto:LaBruzza@bigfoot.com">LaBruzza@bigfoot.
   com</a></center>
<center>Email to José Méndez-Villarubbia at: <a
```

```
href="mailto:MendezVila@aol.com">MendezVila@aol.com
   </a></center>
<!--EndEmail-->

<!–Freetext–>
<p>
This site was rated by Mental Health Net and received its
   Review Badge of Excellence.
<center><a href="http://www.cmhc.com"> <img
   src="http://members.aol.com/tonylouis/home/
   Mhnet. gif" align=middle> </center>
<!--EndFreetext-->
<p>

<!--Counter-->
<center>Number of Visitors at this site is
<img src="http://www.dux.ru/counter/nph-counter?
   link=http://members.aol.com/tonylouis/home/
   dsm.htm&number=6&style=ARIALB&">
<center>

<!--EndCounter-->

</body>

</html>
```

7

DIRECTORY OF USEFUL INTERNET SITES FOR MENTAL HEALTH PROFESSIONALS

This directory compiles various Web pages and Internet resources into broad categories for easy reference. When relevant, it quotes the page's self-description from its Internet site. Some references are repeated under various categories for the reader's convenience. This is a selective list that reflects the author's choice of representative pages from the thousands of mental health sites on the Internet. Commercial sites have been kept to a minimum, and a sampling of the major schools of thought and clinical approaches to patient care has been included.

If you are not sure where to start your Web browsing, try my home page at **http://members.aol.com/tonylouis/home/dsm.htm**. Other good starting points are Mental Health Net at **http://www.cmhc.com/**, HotBot at **http://www.hotbot.com/**, or any of the search engines listed in this directory. The search engines allow you to enter keywords to locate relevant pages on the Internet.

Web sites frequently change their URL addresses as they move from one host computer to another on the Net. If a particular address on this list does not work, do a search for the keywords and you are likely to find its new address. Many sites can also be found on resource pages that provide links to other sites. To highlight the resource pages in this directory, I have capitalized the word LINKS throughout. If you have suggestions for additions or amendments to this list, please e-mail your comments to me at **LaBruzza@pol.net**.

Abuse, Rape, Trauma, and Survival

Warning! Some of the material on the following pages deals with sexual and physical abuse and survivor issues. Some of these discussions may be found to be indecent or offensive according to certain community standards. Explicit discussions of sexual abuse (using "obscene, lewd, lascivious, filthy" language) on the Internet may subject the mental health professional or abused individual to be "be fined under title 18, United States Code, or imprisoned not more than two years, or both" under the provisions of the Exon/Gorton Communications Decency Act of 1996. The complete text of this act can be found on the Web at **http://www.cpsr.org/cpsr/nii/cyber-rights/web/cda/cda.final.html** and it may have been declared unconstitutional by the Supreme Court by the time this book goes to press.

David Baldwin's Trauma Info Pages at **http://gladstone.uoregon.edu/~dvb/trauma.htm**

Child Abuse Yellow Pages at **http://idealist.com/cayp/**

Firewheel Vortex, a man with Dissociative Identity Disorder (multiple personality) tells his story at **http://netpsych.com/web.htm**

The Fly's Abuse/Survivor Resources at
http://freenet.msp.mn.us/people/kaplan/abuse.htm

Patricia D. McClendon's Clinical Social Work Home Page contains many useful LINKS for trauma survivors at
http://www.users.mis.net/~patmc/

Ritual Abuse & Healing Home Page at
http://www.iceonline.net/vortex/rainbow/

Sexual Assault Information Page (with many helpful LINKS to other sites) at
http://www.cs.utk.edu/~bartley/saInfoPage.html

Survivorship: An International Forum on Survival of Ritual Abuse, Torture, & Mind Control at
http://www.iceonline.net/vortex/svship/home.htm

Tesserae: a person with Dissociative Identity Disorder (multiple personality) tells her story of abuse at
http://users.deltanet.com/~tess/index1.html

The Wounded Healer, a resource for survivors of abuse, including professionals who are abuse survivors, at
http://idealist.com/wounded_healer/index.shtml

Addiction Information and Support Services

Al-Anon and Alateen on the Web offers information in several languages at
http://www.A1-Anon-Alateen.org

Alcoholics Anonymous (AA) on the Web at
http://www.alcoholics-anonymous.org/factfile/aafactfi.html

American Academy of Family Physicians Health Notes from Your Family Doctor on "Alcohol, What to do if it's a Problem for You" at
http://www.housecall.com/sponsors/aafp/topics/addiction/alcohol/page0.html

Cocaine Anonymous at **http://www.ca.org/**

Drug-Free Reource Net at **http://www.drugfreeamerica.org/**

Habit Smart: "This Web site has been constructed to provide an abundance of information about addictive behavior: theories of habit endurance and habit change as well as tips for effectively managing problematic habitual behavior." at **http://www.cts.com/~habtsmrt/index.html**

Internet Addiction Disorder at **http://www.cmhc.com/guide/iad.htm**

Internet Addiction Support Group: Send e-mail to **listserv@netcom.com**, leave the subject line blank, and for the body text type: subscribe i-a-s-g

Twisted by Carl Richmond, reviews of a book about addiction and recovery, at **http://pantheon.cis.yale.edu/~rickg/richmond.html**

Web of Addictions Page at **http://www.well.com/user/woa**

AIDS and HIV

AIDS Virtual Library has many useful LINKS and is the place to start when looking for information about AIDS and HIV, at **http://planetq.com/aidsvl/index.html**

The Body, A Multimedia AIDS and HIV Information Resource at **http://www.thebody.com/cgi-bin/body.cgi**

The Center for Disease Control (CDC) Clearinghouse "collects, analyzes, and places information on a wide variety of HIV/AIDS-related subjects into specialized databases" at **http://www.cdcnac.org/database.html**

Dr. Jim Weinrich's AIDS and Sexology home page at **http://math.ucsd.edu/~weinrich/**

The HIV Drug Book (except about psychoactive drugs) at **http://www.thebody.com/pinf/drugbkix.html**

Immunet has links to information about HIV/AIDS at **http://www.immunet.org/**

Search AIDSLINE for Free at **http://www.medscape.com/Medscape/public/announcements/FreeAIDSLINESearching.html**

Alzheimer's Disease

The Alzheimer's Association is "the National Voluntary Health Agency dedicated to researching the preventions, cures and treatments of Alzheimer's disease and related disorders, and providing support and assistance to afflicted patients and their families" at **http://www.alz.org/**

Alzheimer Web at **http://werple.mira.net.au/~dhs/ad.html**

Parke-Davis Alzheimer's Family Care Page: "If you have questions about Alzheimer's disease and wish to speak to someone at no charge, we encourage you to call our Alzheimer's FamilyCare TM line at 1-800-600-1600" at **http://alzheimers.familycare.com/**

The Whole Brain Atlas Keith Johnson's LINKS to Alzheimer sites at **http://count51.med.harvard.edu/AANLIB/khotlist.html**

American Civil Liberties Union (ACLU) Freedom Network

to protect your civil rights at **http://www.aclu.org/**

Anxiety, Panic, and Phobic Disorders

The Anxious Advocate ("make your voice heard on issues affecting people with anxiety disorders") includes LINKS to political sites at **http://www.algy.com/anxiety/advocate.html#2**

The Cyberspace Stress Doc, by L. John Mason, Ph.D., has articles on anxiety, panic, chronic pain, etc. at **http://www2.dstress.com/dstress/jmarticle.html**

National Panic/Anxiety Disorder Newsletter at **http://spiderweb.com/npadnews/quest.htm**

APA (American Psychological Association) Publication Style

APA Publication Manual Crib Sheet is "a summary of rules from the APA Publication Manual" at **http://www.gasou.edu/psychweb/tipsheet/apacrib.htm**

Archie, FTP, Finger, and Telnet Resources

(If you know the name of a specific file, use Archie searches to locate it on the Net.)

Archie Request Form at **http://hoohoo.ncsa.uiuc.edu/archie.html**

Archie Services, a Public Service provided by NEXOR, "is a list of Archie services (gateways) in the World Wide Web"—excellent and comprehensive—at **http://www.nexor.co.uk/archie.html/**

Bowling Green State University Archie Help page at **http://www.bgsu.edu/departments/tcom/archie.html**

FTP (Mining the Net, part II), a helpful explanation of FTP with lots of LINKS to FTP sites, at **http://www.hcc.hawaii.edu/bdgtti/bdgtti-1.02_11.html#SEC119**

NASA Lewis Research Center ArchiePlex, an Archie gateway for the World Wide Web, at **http://www.lerc.nasa.gov/archieplex/**

The Rutgers University Archie Request Form, to search for specific files whose names you know (not for general searches) at **http://ns2.rutgers.edu/htbin/archie**

Telnet (Mining the Net, part I), a useful explanation of Telnet and Finger, at **http://www.hcc.hawaii.edu/bdgtti/bdgtti-1.02_10.html**

Ask a Question about Mental Health Online

1 Online Service "allows direct e-mail access to a full-time staff of top clinical psychotherapists, psychiatrists and experts in addictions, education and family life ready to review and comment on almost any important question or conflict in your life" at **http://www.response-net.com/1xlor.htm**

HelpNet: "Accomplished psychologists and psychiatrists from many specialties, online to answer your questions. Do you have a problem or concern? A question about yourself or someone else? We will answer your questions quickly, professionally, and confidentially" at **http://www.ottawa.net/~helpnet/** or **http://130.212.14.25/helpnet/index.html**

National Panic Anxiety Disorders Newsletter at **http://spiderweb.com/npadnews/quest.htm**

Attention Deficit Hyperactivity Disorder

ADD/ADHD Toronto: "This page is intended as a resource for adolescents, adults, and the parents of children with Attention Deficit Disorder (ADD) or Attention Deficit Hyperactivity Disorder (ADHD)" at **http://www.add-toronto.org/home.html**

ADD Clinic where "we plan to present comprehensive, detailed, and current information about: Attention Deficit Disorder (ADD), Attention Deficit Hyperactivity Disorder (ADHD), Obsessive Compulsive Disorder (OCD), and Tourette Syndrome (TS)" at **http://www.addclinic.com/index.html**

Attention Deficit Disorder WWW Archive with useful LINKS at **http://www.seas.upenn.edu/~mengwong/add/**

HealthGuide: ADHD at **http://206.31.218.3/adhd/**

Books, Book Publishers, and Distributors

Amazon Books Online ("Search one million titles. Enjoy consistently low prices"), at **http://amazon.com/**

American Psychiatric Press at **http://www.appi.org/**

American Psychological Association books at **http://www.apa.org/books/**

Any Psych Book ("Search our 50,000 book catalogue") at **http://www.behavior.net/AnyPsych/**

Book Bargains on some mental health texts at **http://www.behavior.net/bookbargains/**

Cambridge University Press at
http://www.cup.org/Default.html

Computer Literacy Bookshops "are real places, not just a virtual space! Since 1983 we have been providing customers worldwide with the best selection of computer and electronics books and the most knowledgeable service anywhere" (if they do say so themselves) at **http://www.clbooks.com/**

Houghton Mifflin Interactive at **http://www.hminet.com**

Jason Aronson Inc., the publisher of this book, at
http://www.aronson.com

MedSmart, a large mail order medical book seller, at
http://www.lb.com/medsmart/

On-Line Books Page ("Look here for an index of thousands of online books") at
http://www.cs.cmu.edu/books.html

Public domain texts on the Web—the full text of *The Interpretation of Dreams* by Sigmund Freud and of *The Varieties of Religious Experience* by William James can be found at
http://www.gasou.edu/psychweb/books/index.htm

Williams & Wilkins at **http://www.wwilkins.com**

Chat Rooms and Chats

I-Link LINKS to chat rooms at
http://www.ili.net/chat/index.html

WebChat at **http://wbs.net/**

Computers In Mental Health

Computers In Mental Health (CIMH) at
http://www.ex.ac.uk/~mhbrisco/cimh/welcome.htm

Computer Viruses and Computer Support Sites

Anti-Virus Update Center at
http://www.crl.com/%7Ecolocomp/novirus2.htm
Mcafee Anti-Virus at
http://www.mcafee.com/prod/av/av.html
Ray's Win95 Support, Upgrades, and Fixes at
http://www2.gc.net/rwclements/
Shareware.com for finding shareware on the Net at
http://www.shareware.com/

Continuing Education

Many sites list meetings or provide online opportunities to obtain continuing education credits. Some even allow you to listen to case discussions on your computer's speakers. Here are some education sites that look promising.

American Educational Institute, Inc. (AEI) is a commercial continuing education service that offers medical, dental, and legal seminars at various locations, at **http://www.aeiseminars.com**, e-mail at **aei@ix.netcom.com**, telephone (800) 354-3507
Continuing Education for Psychologists:
http://www.webcom.com/paragon/ceweb.html
Doctors' Guide to the Internet at
http://www.pslgroup.com/DOCGUIDE.HTM
Globewide Network Academy, "helping you with distance education, with over ten thousand courses and degree programs listed" at **http://www.gnacademy.org:8001/uu-gna/index.html**, or via e-mail at **gna@uu-gna.mit.edu**

Harvard Medical School:
http://www.med.harvard.edu/conted/

National University Degrees Consortium of "13 accredited universities across the United States working together to offer over 1,000 courses, 3 credit certificates, 11 bachelor's degrees, and 24 graduate degrees through distance education" at (case-sensitive URL)
http://www.ColoState.EDU/Depts/NUDC/

NYU Post-Graduate Medical School Website at
http://www.scanet.com/nyupgms/

Physicians' Forum lists upcoming medical and psychiatric conferences and gives summaries of recent conferences at **http://www.craigusa.com/**

Physicians Online Network (see Physicians Online)

Copyright Information

ClariNet * Brad Templeton Home Page * "A brief intro to copyright" at
http://www.clari.net/brad/copyright.html

The Copyright Website by Benedict O'Mahoney at
http://www.benedict.com/

The Legal Information Institute of Cornell University at
http://www.law.cornell.edu/topics/copyright.html

United States Copyright Office of the Library of Congress at **http://lcweb.loc.gov/copyright/**

Databases and Sources of Mental Health Information

The American Academy of Child and Adolescent Psychiatry (AACAP) offers its award-winning "Facts for Families." "The Academy publishes these 46 information sheets, which provide concise and up-to-date material on issues such as the depressed child, teen suicide, stepfamily problems, and child sexual abuse." These sheets are also available in Spanish and French, at **http://www.aacap.org/web/aacap/factsFam/**

America's HouseCall Network, a "source for health information" at **http://www.housecall.com/index.html**

Behavior Online ("the gathering place for mental health and applied behavioral science professionals") at **http://www.behavior.net/**

Center for Clinical Research Information at **http://www.telemedical.com/~drcarr/Telemedical/crt.html**

Cognitive and Psychological Sciences on the Internet at **http://matia.stanford.edu/cogsci/**

Depression Resources List Compiled and maintained by Dennis Taylor at **http://www.execpc.com/~corbeau/**

Dr. Bob's Virtual En-psych-lopedia at **http://uhs.bsd.uchicago.edu/~bhsiung/tips/tips.html**

The Genome Database Hosted by Johns Hopkins University School of Medicine (for genetics researchers) at **http://gdbwww.gdb.org/**

HealthGuide OnLine: "We offer organized, reliable and accurate health information to you, the Health Care Consumer," at **http://www.healthguide.com/**

Herbal Reference Library at **http://www.all-natural.com/herbindx.html**

HospitalWeb, a list of hospitals on the Web: "Providing a simple and globally accessible way for patients, medical researchers, and physicians to get information on any hospital in the world is the goal" at **http://neuro-www.mgh.harvard.edu/hospitalweb.nclk**

Internet Mental Health Encyclopedia, an excellent resource that is "a free encyclopedia of mental health information. Our hope is that Internet Mental Health will promote improved understanding, diagnosis, and treatment of mental illness throughout the world." **http://www.mentalhealth.com/copy.html**

McLean Hospital Online "bringing a universe of mental health knowledge to you" at **http://www.mcleanhospital.org**

Medscape "membership is free. Once you have registered and have a member name and password, you have full access to all of Medscape's content, including: • Thousands of full-text, peer-reviewed clinical articles • Free access to MEDLINE, the world's largest medical abstract database, and AIDSLINE • Daily medical news updates • Self-assessment features • Word or phrase searching on articles, medical news, discussion group archives, and patient information • Continuing Medical Education resources • Medscape's weekly MedPulse e-mail 'what's new' newsletter." Register at **http://www.medscape.com/misc/formmedlineInfLive.html**

Mental Health Net with thousands of mental health links at **http://www.cmhc.com**

National Clearing House for Alcohol and Drug Information (NCADI) is "the information service of the Center for Substance Abuse Prevention of the U.S. Department of Health & Human Services. NCADI is the world's largest resource for current information and materials concerning substance abuse prevention" at **http://www.health.org/aboutn.htm**

National Institutes for Health (NIH) at **http://www.nih.gov**

The National Mental Health Services Knowledge Exchange Network has LINKS to many databases and mental health resources at **http://www.mentalhealth.org/**

The National Mental Health Services Knowledge Exchange Network also has a toll-free voice number for information at 1-800-789-2647 (CMHS) and an electronic Bulletin Board Service that your modem can call at 1-800-790-2647 (CMHS) for mental health information.

PharmInfonet Drug Information Database at **http://pharminfo.com/drg_mnu.html**

Psych Central, Dr. John Grohol's Mental Health Page, "your personalized one-stop index for psychology, support, and mental health issues, resources, and people on the Internet," at **http://www.coil.com/~grohol/**

The Psychology Web Archive, "Jumping Off Place for Social Psychologists: This public noncommercial site shows LINKS to psychology related resources available on the Internet (World Wide Web and Gopher). The LINKS listed here are mostly focusing on social psychology issues, but take also other psychological topics in consideration (e.g. clinical psychology)" at **http://www.swix.ch/clan/ks/CPSP1.htm**

Search the Virtual Hospital (do a keyword search for articles and information) at **http://www.vh.org/Misc/Search.html**

The Sexuality Library, with dozens of LINKS to resources on human sexuality, at **http://weber.u.washington.edu/~sfpse/ftpsite.html**

U.S. Pharmacopeia Search For Drug Information (just type in the name of the drug and receive an informative description of its effects and indications) at **http://www.housecall.com/databases/usp_di/**

Death, Dying, Grief, and Bereavement

GriefNet, "a collection of resources of value to those who are experiencing loss and grief," at **http://rivendell.org/**

Depression and Bipolar Disorder

The Bipolar Patient at **http://www.tcnj.edu/~ellisles/BipolarPlanet/**

Depression FAQs (Frequently Asked Questions) at **http://www.psych.helsinki.fi/~janne/asdfaq/**

Depression Resources List Compiled and maintained by Dennis Taylor at **http://www.execpc.com/~corbeau/**

HealthGuide: Depression at **http://www.healthguide.com/dep/**

Manic Depression Primer at **http://chandra.cis.brown.edu/bipolar/**

The Uni/Bipolar Disorders Page "reports on different types of depression, their symptoms, possible treatments and drugs. . . . Access to the Option Institute and the Fellowship, a centre that helps to improve the quality of life of families, groups or people" at **http://www.duke.edu/~ntd/depression.html**

Diagnosis

DSM-IV Codes listed by name and number at **http://uhs.bsd.uchicago.edu/dr-bob/tips/dsm4.html**

ICD-9-CM International Classification of Diseases at **http://econ-www.newcastle.edu.au/hsrg/hypertexts/icd9cm.html**

ICD-9-CM Mental Disorders Codes at **http://econ-www.newcastle.edu.au/hsrg/hypertexts/icd9cm_group5.html**

Internet Mental Health at **http://www.mentalhealth.com/copy.html**

Disability Resources

Disability Resources on the Internet at **http://www.disability.com/cool.html**

U.S. Department of Justice Americans with Disabilities Act Home Page at **http://www.usdoj.gov/crt/ada/adahom1.htm**

Discussion Groups of Mental Health Topics

Behavior OnLine: "Behavior OnLine is a gathering place for professionals in mental health and the applied social and behavioral sciences. At this time all Behavior OnLine services and features are provided without charge and access is open to all who are interested. In the future BOL intends to charge for some of its services and to restrict access to some of them," at **http://www.behavior.net/**

Eating Disorders

Anorexia Information and Guidance for Patients, Family, and Friends by Cheryl A. Wildes with useful LINKS at **http://www.neca.com/~cwildes/**

Ask the Dietitian about Anorexia Nervosa, by Joanne Larsen, M.S., R.D., L.D., at **http://www.dietitian.com/anorexia.html**

Cath's LINKS to Eating Disorders resources on Internet at **http://www.stud.unit.no/studorg/ikstrh/ed/**

Educational Resources, Dictionaries, General Reference, Libraries

ARTFL Project: ROGET'S Thesaurus Search Form at **http://humanities.uchicago.edu/forms_unrest/ROGET.html**

Association for Support of Graduate Students at **http://www.asgs.org/**

Bartlett's Familiar Quotations at **http://www.cc.columbia.edu/acis/bartleby/bartlett/**

The Elements of Style by William Strunk, Jr., at **http://www.cc.columbia.edu/acis/bartleby/strunk/**

The Internet Public Library at **http://ipl.sils.umich.edu/**

Kaplan's Student Choice Award-Winning Sites, "a complete list of Kaplan's award-winning Student Choice sites, the

most useful educational resources on the Web" at
http://www.kaplan.com/library/student_sites.html

LINKS to Scholarly Journals on the Web from the University of Houston Libraries at
http://info.lib.uh.edu/wj/webjour.html

Medicine Net Dictionary at
http://www.medicinenet.com/

Mirriam-Webster Online Word of the Day—improve your vocabulary and link to online dictionary at
http://www.m-w.com/cgi-bin/mwwod.pl

On-Line Books Page ("Look here for an index of thousands of online books") at
http://www.cs.cmu.edu/books.html

The Periodic Table of Elements at
http://mwanal.lanl.gov/CST/imagemap/periodic/periodic.html

The Time Service Department, U.S. Naval Observatory, is the official source of time used in the United States and gives the exact time at
http://tycho.usno.navy.mil/time.html

A Web of Online Dictionaries (LINKS to many dictionaries and thesauri online) at
http://www.bucknell.edu/~rbeard/diction.html

WorldWide Classroom is "a compilation of intercultural and educational programs around the world which welcomes international visitors" at
http://www.worldwide.edu/

E-Mail via Telephone—see Phone Facilitators

Fax Number Directories

InfoSpace Fax Directory at **http://in-103.infospace.com/fax**

World Email Directory Business, Phone, and Fax Directories at **http://worldemail.com//wede4ab.shtml**

Finances and Financial Information

American Finance & Investment, Inc., "everything you need to know to make the right decision when it comes to getting the best mortgage" at **http://www.loanshop.com/**

Discussion and Reviews of Computer Billing And Office Management Programs at **http://www.cmhc.com/guide/pro24.htm**

Psychotherapy Finances Home Page Managed Care Strategies—"a publication dedicated entirely to managed care topics of interest to behavioral health practitioners" at **http://www.psyfin.com/**

Finger (not on your hand, the Internet kind)

WWW Finger Gateway ("Reverse Search: Check a person behind an e-mail address") at **http://www-bprc.mps.ohio-state.edu/cgi-bin/finger.pl**

Forensic Psychiatry and Psychology

Forensic Psychiatry Online at **http://www.priory.com/forpsy.htm**

Psychiatry & the Law on Mental Health Net at **http://www.cmhc.com/law/**

FTP (File Transfer Protocol) Sites

Monster FTP Sites List at **http://hoohoo.ncsa.uiuc.edu/ftp/**

SUNET's, the Swedish University Network's, FTP archive at **http://ftp.sunet.se/**

Washington University Data Archive FTP Site "currently contains over 72 gigabytes of space for files" at **http://wuarchive.wustl.edu/**

Gophers, Gopher Sites, and Searches

Galaxy search engine of Web, Gopher, Telnet Resources at **http://galaxy.einet.net/cgi-bin/wais-text-multi**

Gopher root at CWIS at **gopher://cwis.usc.edu/**

Gopher root at University of Minnesota at **gopher://gopher.tc.umn.edu/** (Go here and click on "Other Gopher Information and Servers" to get a list of all the Gopher Servers in the World and for access to Veronica and to WAIS-based information.)

Gophers, WAISs, and the World Wide Web, a helpful explanation, at **http://www.hcc.hawaii.edu/bdgtti/bdgtti-1.02_12.html**

Rice University Gopher directory at **gopher://riceinfo.rice.edu/11/Subject**

Grants and Research Funding

Community of Science Web Server at **http://cos.gdb.org**

Guides to What's Happening on the Web

(These are like *TV Guide* magazines for the Web)

CNET's Events This Week at
http://www.cnet.com/Content/Features/Events/
NetGuide Live at **http://www.netguide.com/**
Timecast at **http://www.timecast.com**
USA Today Cyberlisting at
http://www.usatoday.com/life/cyber/cy.htm
Yahoo's Net Events at **http://events.yahoo.com/**

History and Philosophy of Psychology

Mind And Body: René Descartes To William James, an historical essay by Robert H. Wozniak (Ph.D, Psychology, University of Michigan, 1966) Professor of Psychology at Bryn Mawr College at **http://serendip.brynmawr.edu/Mind/Table.html**
Mind/Brain at
http://mind.phil.vt.edu/www/mind.html

Holistic Mental Health Resources—see New Age, Alternative Medicine, and Holistic Approaches

Home Pages and E-mail for Free

By following fairly straightforward instructions, you should be able to set up your own home page at one of these sites. Once you get your home page up and running, you will want to let the rest of cyberspace know about it by contacting a Web submission site like the one at **http://204.57.42.244/submit.htm**

Angelfire Free Home Pages at
http://www.angelfire.com/
Bigfoot Free E-mail for Life at
http://www.bigfoot.com/BFLife/bfl.htm
Create Your Own Web Site (place a small ad for yourself) at **http://www.inc.com/createsite/**
Four 11 Free E-mail at **http://four11.com/**
Geocities Free Home Pages at
http://www.geocities.com/
InfoSpace Free E-mail at **http://www.infospace.com/**
Juno Free Internet E-Mail Service (telephone 1-800-654-JUNO for a copy of the software) at
http://www.juno.com/
USA Online Free Family or Personal Home Page at
http://www.usaol.com/freeFamilyPage.html
WebChat Free Home Pages at **http://wbs.net/**

Homosexuality—see Sexuality

HTML: Hypertext Markup Language and Editors

Diseño HTML at
http://www.yi.com/home/PerdigueroEusebio/html.htm
Editing Tools for Windows at
http://www.swifty.com/VB/cone/soft/pceditor.htm

HotDog Web Editor at
http://www.sausage.com/dogindex.htm
ICOM LINKS to downloading Internet-related software including Web editors at
http://www.icomkorea.com/compint.html
Improving Your HTML Skills with LINKS and tutorials at
http://linux.usis.bkc.lv/archive/seminar1/htmhelp.htm
LINKS to information about HTML including tutorials and a glossary at **http://207.155.15.117/**
Mag's Big List of HTML Editors, a superb resource at
http://union.ncsa.uiuc.edu/HyperNews/get/www/html/editors.html
Web-It at **http://www.lincolnbeach.com/**

Internet ServiceProviders (ISPs)

ISP Finder, "the easy way to find a local service provider," at **http://www.ispfinder.com/**
Juno Free Internet E-Mail Service (just for e-mail) at
http://www.juno.com/

Internet Tutorials, Glossaries, Guides, and Reference

Doctor's Guide to the Internet at
http://www.pslgroup.com/docguide.htm
Browsing: Beyond the Basics, an Internet tutorial at
http://training.cit.cornell.edu/courses/BeyondBrowsing/WebRes.html
EFF's Extended Guide to the Internet at
http://www.eff.org/papers/eegtti/eeg_toc.html

Glossary of Computer/Internet Terms by Joe Burns, Ph.D., at **http://207.155.15.117/glossary.html**

How to Use Gopher (free course online) at **gopher://cwis.usc.edu/11/Other_Gophers_and_Information_Resources/Gopherin**

The ILC Glossary of Internet Terms at **http://www.matisse.net/files/glossary.html**

Impact Online's Internet 101: Introduction to the Internet, a Course for Nonprofit Organizations, is a useful overview of the Internet for anyone at **http://www.impactonline.org/internet/**

Jack Nelson's Internet Tutor, at **http://www.i-tutor.com/**

Learn the Net Tutorial (available in English, French, Spanish, and Italian), at **http://www.learnthenet.com/**

The McGraw-Hill Internet Training Manual Internet Glossary at **http://www.marketing-coach.com/mh-guide/glossary.htm**

Ohio State University's Internet Tutor, at **http://gateway.lib.ohio-state.edu/tutor/instructions.html**

Psychiatry Navigates the Web, an introductory essay about psychiatry and the WWW by Milton P. Huang, M.D. and Norman Alessi, M.D. © 1995 *Psychiatric Times*. Reprinted with permission, at **http://www.psych.med.umich.edu/web/psytimes/psychwww.htm**

QUE'S Computer and Internet Dictionary: Available to America Online members.

Job Hunting, Employment and Career Opportunities

Career Path, "Help Wanted Ads From Across the Country," at **http://www.careerpath.com/**

Career Magazine online at **http://www.careermag.com/careermag/**

Job Search LINKS to many job related sites at **http://hortpc20.hort.purdue.edu/job.htm**

MedSearch America "is the first and only Internet employment advertising and communications network designed specifically for the healthcare industry," at **http://www.medsearch.com/** or **http://www.neoh.com/jnmsabot.htm**

Mental Health Net—Professional Employment Resources, a "comprehensive listing of professional employment information and professional resources online," at **http://www.cmhcsys.com/guide/pro04.htm**

Monster Board Job Search at **http://www.monster.com/**

Purdue University Placement Service, in West Lafayette, Indiana, "maintains the Internet's largest list of job searching web site," at **http://www.ups.purdue.edu/Student/jobsites.htm**

The Riley Guide Employment Opportunities and Job Resources on the Internet at **http://www.jobtrak.com/jobguide/**

Journals and Professional Newspapers

For a comprehensive list of online journals and newsletters, go to **http://gort.ucsd.edu/newjour/toc.html**

American Journal of Psychotherapy, at
http://www.ajp.org/

American Psychologist, "Integrative articles that draw upon diverse areas of the field and relate them to the whole" at **http://www.apa.org/journals/amp.html**

APA Monitor, "Official newspaper of the American Psychological Association" at
http://www.apa.org/journals/mon.html

Archives of Neurology, at
http://www.ama-assn.org/public/journals/neur/neurhome.htm

Archives of Psychiatric Nursing, at
http://www.wbsaunders.com
telephone (800) 654-2432.

Behavioral & Brain Sciences, at
http://www.cogsci.soton.ac.uk/bbs/

Biotechnology Journals Links at
http://www.bio.com/news/journals.html

Canadian Journal of Psychiatry, "A forum for a broad spectrum of original scholarly presentations, case reports, position papers, editorial contributions, book reviews, and current perspectives" at
http://cpa.medical.org/cpa/public2/publications/cjpintro.htm

Child Development Abstracts and Bibliography, "publishes abstracts and book reviews of research literature selected from about 275 English and foreign-language journals, technical reports, and books that cover education and the biomedical and behavioral sciences," at
http://www.journals.uchicago.edu/CDAB/home.html

Clinical Psychiatry News, e-mail editor at **cpnews@imng.com**

Contemporary Psychology, at **http://www.apa.org/journals/cnt.html**

Gestalt! (eJournal), "A chronicle of the developing application of Gestalt principles," at **http://rdz.stjohns.edu/gestalt!/masthead/**

The Harvard Brain, "Harvard's Undergraduate Neuroscience Magazine," at **http://hcs.harvard.edu/~husn/BRAIN/index.html**

Harvard Mental Health Letter, "Combines a review of the professional literature with original and often controversial articles by experts in all areas of mental health theory, treatment and research," at **http://www.med.harvard.edu/publications/Mental/.index.html**

The International Journal of Psycho-Analysis, at **http://www.ijpa.org/**

International Journal of Psychopathology, Psychopharmacology, and Psychotherapy (eJournal), "devoted to innovations in the understanding of psychopathology and in the psychopharmacologic and psychotherapeutic techniques," at **http://www.psycom.net/ijppp.html**

Journal of the American Medical Association, at **http://www.ama.assn.org**

Journal of Behavior Analysis and Therapy (eJournal), at **http://sage.und.nodak.edu/org/jBAT/jbatinfo.html**

Journal of Clinical Psychoanalysis, at **http://plaza.interport.net/nypsan/jcp.html**

Journal of Cognitive Rehabilitation, at **http://www.inetdirect.net/nsp/**

Journal of Homeopathic Medicine, at **http://204.181.198.34/HomeopathyOnLine/**

Journal of Psychiatry & Neuroscience, "publishes original research articles and review papers in clinical psychiatry (adult and child) and neuroscience related to major psychiatric disorders," at **http://cpa.medical.org/cpa/public2/publications/jpnintro.htm**

Journal of Psychology and the Behavioral Sciences, at **http://alpha.fdu.edu/psychweb/JPBS.htm**

The Lancet, at **http://www.thelancet.com/**

LINKS to Psychological Journal Sites, some of which provide full text of articles, at **http://www.wiso.uni-augsburg.de/sozio/hartmann/psycho/jtext.html**

LINKS to Scholarly Journals on the Web from the University of Houston Libraries, at **http://info.lib.uh.edu/wj/webjour.html**

Managed Care Strategies, "a publication dedicated entirely to managed care topics of interest to behavioral health practitioners," at **http://www.psyfin.com/mcs/mcsintro.htm**

Perception, "a scholarly journal reporting experimental results and theoretical ideas ranging over the fields of human, animal, and machine perception," at **http://www.pion.co.uk/perception/index.html**

Psychoanalytic Studies (eJournal), at **http://www.shef.ac.uk/~psysc/psastud/index.html**

Psychiatric News, "Newspaper of the American Psychiatric Association," at **http://www.appi.org/pnews/pnhome.html**

Psychiatric Times, at **http://www.mhsource.com/edu/psytimes/date.html**

Psychiatry News, e-mail to editor (Robert J Campbell III M.D.) at **pnews@psych.org**

Psychiatry On-Line, an electronic journal edited by Dr. Ben Green at **http://www.cityscape.co.uk/users/ad88/psych.htm**

Psychiatry on-line (eJournal), at **http://www.priory.co.uk/journals/psych.htm**

PsychNews International (eJournal), at **http://www.mhnet.org/pni/**

Psychoanalytic Studies (eJournal), at **http://www.shef.ac.uk/~psysc/psastud/index.html**

Psycoloquy, a "refereed international, interdisciplinary electronic journal sponsored by the American Psychological Association (APA). *Psycoloquy* publishes target articles and peer commentary in all areas of psychology as well as cognitive science, neuroscience, behavioral biology, artificial intelligence, robotics/vision, linguistics and philosophy," at **http://www.princeton.edu/~harnad/psyc.html**

Science, at **http://science-mag.aaas.org/science/**

Scientific American, at **http://www.sciam.com/**

Traumatology (eJournal), at **http://rdz.stjohns.edu/trauma/traumaj.html**

Jungian (Analytical) Psychology

C. G. Jung, Analytical Psychology, and Culture Page at **http://www.cgjung.com/homepage.html**

Libraries Online

Indexes to libraries and library catalogues at
http://www.cfcsc.dnd.ca/links/lib/catin.html
Library of Congress at **http://ftp.loc.gov/**
Library Servers via WWW "currently lists over 1428 pages from libraries in 62 countries" at
http://sunsite.berkeley.edu/Libweb/
National Library of Canada at
http://www.nlc-bnc.ca/catalog/ecat.htm
Networked Resources in Psychology and Mental Health with LINKS to libraries at
http://plaza.interport.net/nypsan/network.html
Public Library LINKS at
http://192.147.157.51/galaxy/Reference/Libraries/Public.html
WWW Library Catalog Gateways, maintained by Eric Lease Morgan of North Carolina State University at
http://www.lib.ncsu.edu/staff/morgan/alcuin/wwwed-catalogs.html

Lists of (and LINKS to) Mental Health Sites and Resources

These are useful lists of Internet sites that are available about a particular subject.

Arizona Health Sciences Library Catalog—Hypertext access to the Arizona Health Sciences Library (AHSL) catalog at **http://aloe.ahsl.arizona.edu/**
Dr. Bob's Mental Health LINKS at
http://uhs.bsd.uchicago.edu/~bhsiung/mental.html

Global Health Network at
http://www.pitt.edu/HOME/GHNet/

Global Health Net—Women's Health at
http://www.pitt.edu/HOME/GHNet/GHWomen.html

HealthTouch Online "Contains up-to-date information on health, wellness, diseases, and illnesses. Topics include the prevention and treatment information on AIDS, allergy, asthma, dental health, diet and nutrition, drug and alcohol abuse, eye diseases and eating disorders," at
http://www.healthtouch.com/

Jon's Big List of Mental Health Sites, "some great mental health sites I've found (sorry, they're not in alphabetical order yet nor are they sorted by type yet). This page is THE source for mental health LINKS for the Indian Health Service Website" at
http://www.wp.com/74329/mh_sites.html

LINKS to Other Sites is "a listing of some great mental health sites separated by site type" at
http://omhs.mhd.hr.state.or.us/LINKS.htm

List of Internet Resource by Specialty—Mental Health, Psychiatry, Psychology (a good place to start if you are searching for a particular resource on the Web) at
http://www.medi.net.hk/html/psychi.htm

Megalists of Psychology-Related Sites on the Web is a list of Web resources devoted to psychology and mental health at
http://www.gasou.edu/psychweb/resource/megalist.htm

Notes on Mental Illness (with LINKS to Web sites about many mental health diagnoses and topics) at **http://www.webcom.com/pleasant/sarah/mental.html**

Psych LINKS from the Hunter College Psychology Department at **http://maxweber.hunter.cuny.edu/psych/sites.html**

Psych Web "contains lots of psychology-related information for students and teachers of psychology," at **http://www.gasou.edu/psychweb/psychweb.htm**

Psychology Internet Resource List (Pirl), Compiled by David Mahony, Vol 3(A), April, 26, 1995 at **http://www.iscm.ulst.ac.uk/~george/subjects/psychology.html**

The WWW Virtual Library, a "distributed subject catalogue" with LINKS for a host of topics on the Web, can be found at **http://www.w3.org/pub/DataSources/bySubject/Overview.html**

Mailing Lists

HealthAtoZ Home–Mailing Lists at **http://www.healthatoz.com/categories/ML.htm**

Publicly Accessible Mailing Lists compiled by Stephanie da Silva at **http://www.neosoft.com/internet/paml/**

RES-LINKS All-in-One Resource Page at **http://www.cam.org/~intsci/index.html**

The file interest-groups.txt, which you can download via FTP, at **ftp://nisc.sri.com/netinfo/**

Managed Care Problems and Abuses

AAPS (American Association of Physicians and Surgeons), at **http://www2.misnet.com/~rick/**

The HMO Page (includes the Atrocity of the Month and the HMO Hall of Shame), at **http://www.hmopage.org/**

The National Coalition Of Mental Health Professionals & Consumers, a group that is "working to expose, regulate, and replace managed care" at **http://www.execpc.com/~mastery/coalitionMain.html**; telephone, 1-888-SAY-NO-MC (1-888-729-6662)

Medical Resources

Achoo "acts as a jump point and information resource for the medical community and all other Internet users interested in healthcare information" at **http://www.achoo.com/**

Arizona Health Sciences Library Catalog—Hypertext access to the Arizona Health Sciences Library (AHSL) catalog at **http://aloe.ahsl.arizona.edu/**

The Columbia Health Information Site at **http://www.columbia.net/**

Cyberspace Hospital at **http://www.crc.nus.sg/CH/level1.html**

Hardin Meta Directory of Internet Health Resources at **http://www.lib.uiowa.edu/hardin-www/home.html/md.html**

ICOM Medical and Dental LINKS at **http://www.icomkorea.com/lvngmed.html**

The Interactive Patient at Marshall University School of Medicine "is a truly unique Interactive World Wide Web Program that allows the user to simulate an actual patient encounter" at **http://medicus.marshall.edu/medicus.htm**

Medical and Health Websites—"The Internet Address Book of Philip A. Gilly, M.D.," a superb list of LINKS to medical resources at **http://www.albany.net/~kinderhk/medical.htm**

The Multimedia Medical Reference Library at **http://www.med-library.com/**

Reuters Health Information Services (general health and medical) at **http://www.reutershealth.com/**

Stanford's MedWorld with LINKS to medical sites, free MedLine, and a medical search engine at **http://medworld.stanford.edu/medworld/home/index.html**

The Visible Human, dissect a human body online at **http://www.cs.umd.edu/projects/hcil/Research/1995/vhe.html**

Web Doctor, "the Internet Navigator for Health-Care professionals. WebDoctor features a comprehensive, peer-reviewed index of Internet medical resources that is designed to provide up-to-date medical information to practicing physicians" at **http://www.gretmar.com/**

Medicare & Medicaid

Health Care Financing Administration (HCFA), the federal agency that administers the Medicare and Medicaid programs, at **http://www.hcfa.gov/**

Medications, Pharmacy, and Psychopharmacology

Dr. Bob's Virtual En-psych-lopedia (Psychopharmacology Tips) at
http://uhs.bsd.uchicago.edu/~bhsiung/tips/intro.html

Drug Information Search Page at
http://wizard.pharm.wayne.edu/drh/disearch.htm

Food and Drug Administration (FDA) at
http://www.fda.gov

HealthGuide OnLine at **http://www.healthguide.com/** or **http://206.31.218.3/pharmacy/**

Internet Mental Health at
http://www.mentalhealth.com/copy.html

Internet Self Assessment in Pharmacology, quiz yourself at
http://www.cs.umn.edu/Research/GIMME/ISAP/welcome.html

LINKS to many pharmacy-related sites and databases at
http://157.142.72.77/pharmacy/pharmint.html

Medical Sciences Bulletin Drug Reviews at
http://pharminfo.com/pubs/msb/msbmnu.html#msb_top

MedWeb Pharmacy and Pharmacology LINKS at
http://www.gen.emory.edu/medweb/medweb.pharmacy.html

Pharmacy WWW LINKS at
http://157.142.72.77/pharmacy/pharmint.html

PharmInfoNet! offers "a database of drug information browsable by generic name or trade name" and many other types of information at
http://pharminfo.com/

Psychopharmacology Tips by Dr. Robert Hsiung at **http://uhs.bsd.uchicago.edu/dr-bob/tips/tips.html**

Medline Searches for Free

Association of Rhode Island Health Sciences Libraries "Free" Medlines LINKS at **http://www.brown.edu/Facilities/University_Library/beyond/arihsl/medlines.html**

Community of Science Medline Database (this site is excellent) at **http://muscat.gdb.org/repos/medl/**

Free MEDLINE Searching from National Center for Biotechnology Information at **http://www.uhs.wisc.edu/medline.html**

HealthGate at **http://www.healthgate.com/HealthGate/MEDLINE/search.shtml/**

Mental Health Services and Provider Directories Online

DocsOnline is a health care directory that "will enable you to locate dentists, physicians, health care providers, or hospitals in your area based on your specific health care needs. By using DocsOnline you will be able to gather information about a health care provider through our Personal Practice Profiles" at **http://www.docsonline.com/**

NetPsych "explores the uses of the Internet to deliver mental health services. This is a new frontier. There aren't many rules, and questions remain. Other sites are built as directories of real world mental health resources, or as a combination of real world and online resources. NetPsych is the first site to focus exclusively on online resources, at **http://netpsych.com/**

Psychological Consultation over the Net, Pay if it Helps (see NetPsych above): "These are hybrid resources which have web sites but also use other aspects of online or off-line communication. Some of the most creative web sites which deliver services are on this page since it is difficult to deliver some services through the web alone."—NetPsych/Hybrid at **http://netpsych.com/hybrid/htm**

Therapist Directory, a commercial site that may occasionally be useful in locating therapists, presents itself as "a geographically organized list of psychiatrists, psychologists, and social workers" but is a very incomplete listing because therapists must be licensed, have malpractice insurance, and pay $89.95 yearly in this age of managed care to get their names in this directory. (Instead, therapists might consider setting up their own home page at one of the free sites on the Web.) Its address is at **http://www.psychology.com/therapy.htm**

Neurology

The *Journal of Neuroscience* at **http://www.jneurosci.org/**

Neurosciences on the Internet at **http://ivory.lm.com/~nab/#recent**

NeuroWorld, The Online Magazine of Neuromedicine, at **http://www.neurosource.com/NeuroWorld/aaa.html**

Neuropsychology, Neurobiology, Brain and Behavior

The National Academy of Neuropsychology at **http://www.nan.drexel.edu/**

Neuropsychology Central: "The primary objectives of this home page are:

To describe the importance of neuropsychology as a science of brain and behavior

To increase public knowledge of neuropsychology as a branch of practical medicine

To indicate the contribution which neuropsychology is making to the neurosciences

To act as a resource for the professional and lay person, alike." at **http://www.premier.net/~cogito/neuropsy.html**

Neurosciences on the Internet at **http://www.lm.com/~nab/**

NeurXercise Computer-Assisted Cognitive Remediation for Brain-Impaired Individuals (computer exercises for improving cognitive functioning). Send e-mail to **neurx@mail.maxeynet.com**

Serendip Brain and Behavior at **http:// serendip.brynmawr.edu/bb/**

The Whole Brain Atlas ("enables the user to see anatomical images of both normal and diseased brain") at **http://count51.med.harvard.edu/AANLIB/home.html**

New Age, Alternative Medicine, and Holistic Approaches to Mental Health

There is a plethora of new age, holistic, and alternative medicine sites on the Web. Listed below are sites that did not seem to fit into traditional categories.

Alternative Medicine Home Page, "a jump station for sources of information on unconventional, unorthodox, unproven, or alternative, complementary, innovative, integrative therapies," at **http://www.pitt.edu/~cbw/altm.html**

Alternative Medicine Internet And On-Line Resources at **http://www.halcyon.com/libastyr/netbib.html**

American Holistic Medical Association (AHMA) at **http://www.doubleclickd.com/about_ahma.html**

American Holistic Nurses Association (AHNA) at **http://www.ahna.org/index.html**

Esoteric Web Link Index at **http://www.AccessNewAge.com**

Eye Movement Desensitization and Reprocessing at **http://www.emdr.org/**

Herbal Reference Library at **http://www.all-natural.com/herbindx.html**

Jungian Approach to the Tarot at **http://angelfire.com/ct/AnthonyLouis/index.html**

Gestalt Institute of Santa Cruz at **http://www2.ucsc.edu/people/goodlan/index.html**

Holistic Resources Center at **http://www.holisticliving.org/**

Holistic Resources on the WWW (over 200 LINKS to holistic health sites—this is the place to start) at **http://www.samart.co.th/hps/wwwresor.htm**

Logic Connection, a new age site with many useful links to international search engines at **http://www.infobahnos.com/~logic/english.htm**

LyghtForce, "your one-stop source for alternative health information and products" (a site that features homeopathy), at **http://lyghtforce.com/**

Miracles Counseling by Dr. Lori Phelps (e-mail: **lphelps@ earthlink.net**) at **http://websites.earthlink.net/~miraclescounseling/**

Neuro-Linguistic Programming LINKS at **http://www.vitinc.com/pdoa/link11.html**

Prayer Ministry Prayer Line at **http://www.pinn.net/~vbumc/prayer.html**, or send e-mail with a request for prayer to **vbumc@pinn.net**

"PSYCH" Mailing List—"born September 21, 1995, 14:40 BST, London, England, for psychological astrology" (moderator: Dermod Moore). To subscribe send e-mail to: **listserver@astrologer.com** with the message: subscribe psych

Reiki, "(pronounced ray-key) is a method of natural healing based on the application of universal life force energy," at **http://www.crl.com./~davidh/reiki/**

WellNet at **http://wellnet.ca/**

Worldwide Wellness Page ("be well naturally") at **http://www.doubleclickd.com/wwwellness.html**

Newsgroups (Usenet)

HealthAtoZ Home—News Groups at **http://www.healthatoz.com/categories/NG.htm**

RES-LINKS NewsGroups/Mailing Lists at **http://www.cam.org/~intsci/newsmail.html**

Newspapers, Magazines, Radio, TV, and News Services Online

For a comprehensive list of newspapers worldwide, try Online Newspapers, which lists more than 1050 sites. Online Newspapers is "one of the most comprehensive lists of online newspapers available on the Net, listed alphabetically by country and updated daily" at **http://www.webwombat.com.au/intercom/newsprs/index.htm**.

The Boston Globe at **http://www.boston.com/globe/glohome.htm**

CNET.COM for news, computer information, shareware, games, software reviews, and a computer glossary at **http://www.cnet.com/**

CNET Radio on the Web; hear the news at **http://www.news.com/Radio/Rams/1997/02/20/ns.ram**

CNET Television at **http://www.cnet.com/Content/Tv/**

CNN at **http://www.cnn.com/**

Dallas Morning News at **http://www.dallasnews.com/**

ESPN at **http://espnet.sportszone.com/**

Health News from the *New England Journal of Medicine* at **http://www.healthnet.ivi.com/ivi/hnews/common/htm/index.htm**

The International Herald Tribune at **http://www.iht.com/**

Los Angeles Times at **http://www.latimes.com/**

National Geographic at **http://nationalgeographic.com**

NBC at **http://www.nbc.com/**

The New York Times at **http://www.nytimes.com/**

The Newsroom has LINKS to many online sources of news at **http://www.auburn.edu/~vestmon/news.html**

Popular Science at **http://www.popsci.com**

Slate at **http://www.slate.com/**

Time Magazine at **www.pathfinder.com/time/daily** or **http://pathfinder.com@@6@elpgUALIibObuX/time/daily/**

USA Today at **http://www.usatoday.com**

The Washington Post at **http://www.washingtonpost.com/**

Nursing Resources and Organizations

HealthWeb List of Nursing Organizations at **http://www.lib.umich.edu/tml/organ.html**

The American Psychiatric Nurses Association at **http://www.musc.edu/apna/**

Nursing World, Home Page of the American Nurses Association at **http://www.ana.org/**

Obsessive Compulsive Disorder and Tourette's Disorder

ADD Clinic has information on Obsessive Compulsive Disorder (OCD) and Tourette Syndrome (TS) at **http://www.addclinic.com/index.html**

ADD Medical Treatment Center of Santa Clara Valley's "Understanding Attention Deficit Disorder" at **http://www.addmtc.com/tenneur.html**

Parental Guidance: Censoring Children's Access to the Net

The following are some of the commercial programs that allow parents to block objectionable Internet sites from their children's prying eyes. The list is not intended as an endorsement of any particular product. You will need to do your own research and decide which, if any, is for you.

Cyber Patrol at **http://www.cyberpatrol.com** or phone 800-828-2608.
Cybersitter at **http://www.solidoad.com**
Gulliver's Guardian at **http://www.gulliver.nb.ca** or phone 800-561-4124.
Net Nanny at **http://www.netnanny.com**
Net Shepherd at **http://www.shepherd.com**
Specs for Kids at **http://www.newview.com**
Surf Watch at **http://www.surfwatch.com**

Patient Education Materials, Brochures, and Newsletters

AACAP Facts for Families "to educate parents and families about psychiatric disorders affecting children and adolescents," at **http://www.aacap.org/web/aacap/factsFam/**

Doctors' Guide to the Internet at **http://www.pslgroup.com/DOCGUIDE.HTM**

KidsHealth.org offers patient education materials for parents and their children plus a section for health professionals that includes case presentations at **http://kidshealth.org/**

Menninger Clinic Articles on Mental Health (about various mental health problems and disorders) at **http://www.menninger.edu/tmc_artmnt.html**

The National Mental Health Services Knowledge Exchange Network (KEN) provides information about mental health via toll-free telephone services (1-800-789-2647), an electronic bulletin board (1-800-790-2647), and publications; "callers can request a publications list or order articles, booklets, fact sheets, and videos on subjects such as children, adolescents, and their families; community resources; and issues that affect consumers of mental health services. KEN also has information on Federal grants, conferences, and other events." KEN's Internet address is **http://www.mentalhealth.org/about/**

National Panic/Anxiety Disorder Newsletter "is designed to provide information in regard to the subject matter covered. It is provided with the understanding that the editor/publisher is not engaged in rendering medical advice" at **http://spiderweb.com/npadnews/quest.htm**

Psychology in Daily Life: "The Public Affairs Office of the American Psychological Association has prepared several brochures to provide information on mental health and psychological issues that face us all. They're collected into topical groups of work, family and the mind–body connection. You'll also find a list here of state and provincial psychological associations, many of which offer referrals for mental health services, as well as a link to association ethics documents," at **http://www.apa.org/pubinfo/pubinfo.html**

The Student Counseling Virtual Pamphlet Collection provides online information about "alcohol and substance use, anxiety, assertiveness, cults, cultural issues, depression, eating disorders, family issues, relationships, sexual assault, sexual harassment, sexual orientation, sleep, stress, study skills, time management, traumatic events" at **http://uhs.bsd.uchicago.edu/scrs/vpc/vpc.html**

U.S. Pharmacopeia Search For Drug Information and Patient Information Leaflets at **http://www.housecall.com/databases/usp_di/**

People Locators and Searches

Find a colleague or a friend.

Bigfoot at **http://www.bigfoot.com/**
Database America's People Finder at
http://www.databaseamerica.com/html/gpfind.htm
Find-A-Doc: "Aid for patients seeking physicians. Presents information on practice," at **http://findadoc.com**
Find Anything is a compilation of LINKS to various search engines and databases at
http://www.gasou.edu/psychweb/resource/findit.htm
InfoSpace People Finder at **http://www.infospace.com/**
WhoWhere at **http://www.whowhere.com/**
WhoWhere? International Phone Directory Links at
http://www.whowhere.com/wwphone/world.html

Pharmacy and Pharmaceuticals—see Medications

Phone Facilitators

Here is a list of software developers and service providers that offer long-distance phone calls and/or the retrieval of e-mail messages via telephone from locations remote from your desktop computer.

American Network Systems: telephone (805) 579-8898
AT&T Wireless Service: **http://www.airdata.com**
Millennia Softward Email Reader: **http://www.msw.com**
NetSpeak Corporation: **http://www.netspeak.com**
NetPhonic Communications Inc.:
http://www.netphonic.com

Unwired Planet Inc.: **http://www.uplanet.com**
VocalTec Ltd.: **http://www.vocaltec.com**
Willow Pond Corporation: **http://www.willowpond.com**

Physicians Online (POL) Network

POL is a network that is offered free to physicians and for a fee to other professionals. No physician with a computer should be without this service. Its sponsors include many of the pharmaceutical companies, and it offers e-mail, discussion groups, MedLine searches, drug databases, five hours of free Web access per month, online physician recruiting, patient education materials, and more. Information about POL can be obtained from POL, 560 White Plains Road, Tarrytown, NY 10591; telephone (800) 332-0009. The POL Administrative Contact is John Scheffel, e-mail at **jscheffel@pol.net**, phone (914) 322-6100 x266, and fax (914) 332-6445.

Professional Associations, Institutions, and Organizations

A COMPLETE LISTING OF ALL PROFESSIONAL ASSOCIATIONS' Mailing Addresses and Phone Numbers (a superb resource) at **http://www.cmhc.com/guide/pro79.htm**
American Academy of Child and Adolescent Psychiatry (AACAP) at **http://www.aacap.org/web/aacap**
American Holistic Medical Association (AHMA) at **http://www.doubleclickd.com/about_ahma.html**
American Holistic Nurses Association (AHNA) at **http://www.ahna.org/index.html**
American Medical Association at **http://www.ama-assn.org/**

American Psychoanalytic Association at **http://apsa.org**

American Psychological Association Home Page at **http://www.apa.org/**

American Psychiatric Association at **http://www.psych.org/**

American Psychiatric Nurses Association at **http://www.musc.edu/apna/**

American Psychoanalytic Association at **http://apsa.org/**

American Society of Psychoanalytic Physicians at **http://pubweb.acns.nwu.edu/~chessick/aspp.htm**

Association of American Physicians and Surgeons (AAPS), a national organization of physicians dedicated to preserving freedom in the one-on-one patient–physician relationship, at **http://www2.misnet.com/~rick/**

Association of Black Psychologists at **http://www.abpsi.org/**

Association of Gay and Lesbian Psychiatrists at **http://members.aol.com/aglpnat/homepage.html**

C. J. Jung Foundation for Analytic Psychology at **http://www.cgjung.com/nyfound.html**

National Academy of Neuropsychology at **http://www.libertynet.org/~nan/index.html**

National Alliance for the Mentally Ill (NAMI) at **http://www.cais.com/vikings/nami/**

National Association of School Psychologists at **http://www.uncg.edu/~ericcas2/nasp/**

National Federation of Societies for Clinical Social Work, Inc., a "confederation of 35 state societies for clinical social work promoting the highest standards of professional education and clinical practice," at **http://www.nfscsw.org/**

National Institutes of Mental Health at **http://www.nimh.nih.gov/home.htm**

SAMSHA Center for Mental Health Services at **http://www.samhsa.gov/cmhs/cmhs.htm**

SAMSHA Center for Substance Abuse Prevention at **http://www.samhsa.gov/csap/csap.htm**

SAMSHA Center for Substance Abuse Treatment at **http://www.samhsa.gov/csat/csat.htm**

The Society for Computers in Psychology at **http://www.lafayette.edu/allanr/scip.html**

The Substance Abuse and Mental Health Services Administration (SAMHSA) at **http://www.samhsa.gov/**

Psychoanalysis

The Abraham A. Brill Library of New York Psychoanalytic Institute at **http://plaza.interport.net/nypsan/**

American Psychoanalytic Association at **http://plaza.interport.net/nypsan/apa.html**

The Interpretation of Dreams (3rd edition) by Sigmund Freud, translated by A. A. Brill, (1911)—the full text of this public domain classic can be found at **http://www.gasou.edu/psychweb/books/interp/toc.htm**

Psychological Test and Screening Instruments

Buros Institute of Mental Measurements at **http://www.unl.edu/buros/**

Clinical Depression Screening Test—see if you meet criteria for clinical depression online, at **http://sandbox.xerox.com/pair/cw/testing.html**

The Educational Testing Service (ETS) Test Collection database "contains records on over 10,000 tests and research instruments" at **http://ericae2.educ.cua.edu/testcol.htm#trev**

ERIC/AE Test Locator at **gopher://vmsgopher.cua.edu/11gopher_root_eric_ae:[_tc]**

The Keirsey Temperament Sorter by David Keirsey is a personality test that scores results according to the Myers-Briggs system at **http://sunsite.unc.edu/personality/keirsey.html**

M.D. Angus & Associates Ltd., a commercial site that sells psychological tests, at **http://www.psychtest.com/index.html**

MMPI: Bob Gordon's MMPI/MMPI-2/MMPI-A Information Site at **http://www.webcom.com/rmgordon**

Psychology LINKS

Cyber-Psych "is committed to bringing high quality, professional psychological care and information to the online community" and has LINKS to many online mental health resources at **http://www.webweaver.net/psych/**

Indiana University Psychology Jumping Stand at **http://www.indiana.edu/~iuepsyc/PsycJump.html**

Psychotherapy

Guide to Psychotherapy at **http://www.shef.ac.uk/%7Epsysc/psychotherapy/index.html**

HealthGuide: Therapy at **http://206.31.218.3/therapy/**

Quality Assurance and Accreditation

National Committee for Quality Assurance (NCQA) rates health plans at **http://www.ncqa.org**

Reference (General) and Research Tools

City.Net (travel and geographical information) at **http://www.city.net/**

The Library of Congress "offers a wide variety of online databases and Internet resources" at **http://www.loc.gov/**

The New York Public Library at **http://www.nypl.org/**

Online Dictionary of Mental Health of the Guide to Psychotherapy Search Page at **http://www.shef.ac.uk/~psysc/psychotherapy/search.html**

Purdue University's Virtual Reference Desk, "government documents . . . dictionaries, thesauri, acronyms . . . phone books and area codes . . . maps and travel information. A collection of maps as well as travel information . . . periodic tables of elements . . . weights and measures conversion tables. Time and date. A gateway to monthly and yearly calendars . . . ZIP, and international country codes" at **http://thorplus.lib.purdue.edu/reference/index.html**

Research-It!, "Research Types: language . research . geographical . financial . internet . shipping & mailing" at **http://www.itools.com/research-it/research-it.html**

Schizophrenia

HealthGuide: Schizophrenia at
http://206.31.218.3/schiz/

Webtrack in Schizophrenia: "Concise impartial summaries of the latest research and treatment news provided by experts in the field. Readable and brief with references," at
http://www.priory.com/journals/webtrack.htm

Search Engines, Web Directories, and Subject Indices

These are databases that allow you to search by keyword. They are excellent for researching topics on the Internet and a good place to start your exploration of the Internet. A good place to start is "The Searcher," a page with LINKS to the major search engines and directories at
http://cpcug.org/user/jlacombe/search.html.

Achoo "acts as a jump point and information resource for the medical community and all other Internet users interested in healthcare information," at
http://www.achoo.com/

Buscadores en Español (Spanish language search engines for the Net) at
http://www.intercom.es/navegador/busca.htm

Countway Web Catalogue is "a collection of biomedicine-related web sites. All the LINKS to be found in the Countway Web Catalog are that of sites which have been selected by the Francis A. Countway's staff for their quality, versatility, and potential usefulness."

Search for a keyword at **http://www.med.harvard.edu/webjewels/index.html#29**

Demon Internet Query Tools at **http://www.demon.net/external/ntools.html**

Demon Internet Search the Net (LINKS to Alta Vista, Yahoo, Excite, Infoseek, WebCrawler, Lycos, Dejanews, Shareware.com, WhoWhere, and Bigfoot) at **http://www.demon.net/inews/search.html**

Doctor's Guide links to search tools at **http://www.pslgroup.com/SEARCH.HTM**

European Search Engines at **http://www.yweb.com/**

Excite at **http://www.excite.com/**

Find Anything is a compilation of LINKS to various search engines and databases. This is an excellent place to start searching for almost any type of information (e.g., addresses, phone numbers, weather reports, etc.) at **http://www.gasou.edu/psychweb/resource/findit.htm**

Galaxy, "the Web's resources, compiled for professionals," at **http://www.einet.net/**

G.O.D. "stands for the Global On-line Directory and includes Web searching and PeopleFinder" at **http://www.god.co.uk/**

HealthAtoZ Database and Links at **http://healthatoz.com/**

HotBot ("HotBot's crawler is the fastest on earth") at **http://www.hotbot.com/**

I-Link LINKS to Chat Rooms and Search Engines at **http://www.ili.net/**

Infoseek at **http://www2.infoseek.com/index.html**

Lycos at **http://www.lycos.com/**

Magellan Internet Guide at **http://searcher.mckinley.com/searcher/cgi?query=**

MedBot, "the easiest way to search the web for health and medicine resources. Only available from Stanford MedWorld" at **http://www-med.stanford.edu/medworld/medbot/**

Open Text, "Text Management and Retrieval—includes search engines and other text retrieval software, as well as specialized text- and/or document-oriented database management systems," at **http://www.elucidate.com/genquery.cgi?prodcatnum=25**

OZU Spanish Language Web Search Engine at **http://www.ozu.es**

PsychCrawler, a search engine designed to locate mental health information on the Web, at **http://www.psychcrawler.com/plweb-cgi/fastweb**

Psych Journal Search on Mental Health Net at **http://www.cmhc.com/journals/**

Quick Find at Mental Health Net (an excellent research resource): "an instant SEARCH of the largest online catalog of mental health, psychology and psychiatry resources," at **http://www.nfscsw.org/** or **http://www.cmhc.com/mhn/AT-MHNsearch.cgi**

Ray's List of Search Engines at **http://www2.gc.net/rwclements/search.html**

RES-LINKS All-in-One Resource page ("My goal while creating these pages was to help you make the best use of the search tools and utilities available on the Net") is a superb resource at **http://www.cam.org/~intsci/index.html**

Self-Help Sourcebook Online sponsored by Mental Health Net (searches for self-help pages) at **http://www.cmhc.com/selfhelp/**

Starting Point Powersearch provides LINKS to several good search engines at **http://www.stpt.com/cgi-bin/pwrsrch/msla.cgi**

Webcrawler at **http://www.webcrawler.com**

Self-Help and Emotional Support

Breast Cancer Information at **http://nysernet.org/bcic/**

Coping with AIDS and HIV at **http://www.thebody.com/mental.html**

Depression Resources List compiled and maintained by Dennis Taylor at **http://www.execpc.com/~corbeau/**

Emotional Support Guide: Internet Resources for Physical Loss, Chronic Illness, and Bereavement at **http://asa.ugl.lib.umich.edu/chdocs/support/emotion.html**

How to Treat Your Own Panic Disorder at **http://www.eadd.com/~berta/**

Relaxation Response Techniques (instructions on how to elicit the relaxation response) at **http://www.thebody.com/mb/relax.html**

Self-Help & Psychology Magazine at **http://www.cybertowers.com/selfhelp/**

Self-Help Sourcebook Online sponsored by Mental Health Net: "This guide has been developed to act as your starting point for exploring real-life support groups and networks that are available throughout the world and in your community," at **http://www.cmhc.com/selfhelp/**

The Victorian Mental Illness Awareness Council (VMIAC), "based in Melbourne, Australia, is a consumer/survivor-run advocacy organization for people with mental health problems. Its membership includes both consumer/survivor groups and individuals who have experienced difficulties with their mental and/or emotional health. The VMIAC is committed to ensuring greater empowerment for people with mental health problems," at **http://www.vicnet.net.au/~vmiac/home.htm**

Sexuality, Gender, Homosexuality, and Sex Education

Warning! Some of the material on the following pages deals with explicit discussion of sexuality and may be found to be indecent or offensive according to certain community standards. Using "obscene, lewd, lascivious, filthy" language on the Internet may subject the mental health professional to be "be fined under title 18, United States Code, or imprisoned not more than two years, or both" under the provisions of the Exon/Gorton Communications Decency Act of 1996. The complete text of this act can be found on the Web at **http://www.cpsr.org/cpsr/nii/cyberrights/web/cda/cda.final.html** and it may have been declared unconstitutional by the Supreme Court by the time this book goes to press.

American Psychological Association's and the American Medical Association's Positions on Homosexuality at **http://www.geocities.com/WestHollywood/1348/apa_ama.htm**

American Social Health Association, "Mission Statement: Stop sexually transmitted diseases (STDs) and their harmful consequences to individuals, families, and communities," at **http://sunsite.unc.edu/ASHA/**

Association of Reproductive Health Professionals at **http://www.arhp.org/**

Doctor Ruth Online at **http://www.drruth.com/**

Focus International: "Your Sexual Health Education Store will send you professional sex education materials in plain packaging" at **http://www.sex-help.com/index-text.html**

Gender-Web for the transgendered community at **http://travesti.geophys.mcgill.ca/~tstar/index.html**

Homosexuality, Common Questions and Statements Addressed, at **http://www.geocities.com/WestHollywood/1348**

Hunter College Home Page of Lesbian and Gay History, Politics, and Culture with many LINKS at **http://maxweber.hunter.cuny.edu/polsc/ksherrill/eng1860.html**

Just Say Yes "means having a positive attitude about sexuality" at **http://www.positive.org/cps/jsy/jsy.html**

Men on the Net LINKS to information on HIV/AIDS, gay organizations, and gay spirituality at **http://www.menonthenet.com/men8.html**

MenWeb M.E.N. Magazine articles from the viewpoint of the Men's Movement at **http://www.vix.com/menmag/**

Safe Sex educational materials, a Gopher site of NIH documents, at **gopher://gopher.niaid.nih.gov/11/aids/comm/teach**

Sexuality Library with numerous LINKS at **http://weber.u.washington.edu/~sfpse/ftpsite.html**

Yahoo's Society and Culture Sexuality Directory at **http://www.yahoo.com/Society_and_Culture/Sexuality/**

Shareware

Software you can download and test before you buy it.

C/NET's Shareware.com can be used to search for shareware programs on the Net at **http://search.shareware.com/SW/FD/Home/**
Download.com at **http://www.download.com/**
Edepot's Shareware Depot at **http://www.edepot.com/**
Filez Catalogue with links to files at FTP sites at **http://www.filez.com/**
Unicorn Software Download Site at **http://www.unicornsoftware.com/**
WinSite, "the Planet's Largest Software Archive for Windows shareware and trialware on the Internet," at **http://www.winsite.com/about/**

Shopping

iMALL, Inc.—The Largest Retail Web Site With Over 1000 Merchants! at **http://www.imall.com/**
DealerNet if you're planning to buy a car at **http://www.dealernet.com/**
Global Shopping Network International at **http://www.gsni.com/index/htm**
Infoseek Shopping Directory at **http://www2.infoseek.com/Shopping**

The Internet Auction List at
http://www.usaweb.com/auction.html
Onsale Online Auction of Used Computer Equipment at
http://www.onsale.com/

Sleep and Dreams

DreamGate & Electric Dreams Bibliography at
http://www.dreamgate.com/dream/bibs/
HandiLINKS to Sleep and Dreams at
http://www.ahandyguide.com/cat1/s/s615.htm
Sleep Medicine Home Page with many LINKS to sleep-related pages at **http://www.cloud9.net/~thorpy/**
SleepNet, "everything you wanted to know about sleep disorders but were too tired to ask," at
http://www.sleepnet.com/
Yahoo! Science:Psychology:Sleep and Dreams at
http://www.iconn.iphil.net/subcat.ref/online/yahoindx/sci/aau/kat/index.htm

Social Work

The Eugene Social Worker has lots of social work LINKS to the tune of Mission Impossible at
http://www.efn.org/~anthonyg/
The New Social Worker Online at
http://www.xmission.com/~gastown/newsocwk/index.html
Patricia D. McClendon's Clinical Social Work Home Page contains many useful LINKS. "Identifying and communicating effective treatment protocol for trauma survivors is, in part, what I hope this home page accomplishes," at **http://www.users.mis.net/~patmc/**

The Social Worker Networker, "your 'user-friendly' guide to mental health and Internet resources. . . . Please recommend any valuable Internet resources that are not listed here, so that I may add them," at **http://www.accessone.com/~hammer/**

Spanish Language and Culture

Hispanic Online, "the Web site of *HISPANIC* Magazine, a monthly magazine for and about Hispanics with a national circulation of 250,000. We cover news, events, and issues of interest to the Latino Community," at **http://www.hisp.com/**

Latino LINKS at **http://www.hisp.com/LINKS.html**

El Tao de Día, daily quotes in Spanish from the Chinese Classic *Tao Te Ching* by Lao Tsu, at **http://www.ciudadfutura.com/cgi-localbin/horoscopo/tao.pl**

Webspañol "is committed to promoting the study and appreciation of the Spanish Language by utilizing every available internet resource," at **http://www.geocities.com/Athens/Acropolis/7409/**

Stress Management and Meditation

The Cyberspace Stress Doc has LINKS and articles on stress and anxiety at **http://www2.dstress.com/dstress/jmLINKS.html**

HealthGuide: Stress at **http://www.healthguide.com/stress/**

Relaxation Response Techniques (instructions on how to elicit the relaxation response) at **http://www.thebody.com/mb/relax.html**

Relaxation Techniques from Noodles' Panic-Anxiety Page at **http://www.algy.com/anxiety/relax.html**

Stress, Anxiety, and Depression Information LINKS at **http://www.thebody.com/mental.html#stress**

Stress Management and Relaxation, "a WWW-tutorial on Progressive Muscle Relaxation, information on the Mantra Meditation technique," at **http://ourworld.compuserve.com/homepages/har/relax.htm**

Suicide, Para-Suicide, and Self-Mutilation

Frequently Asked Questions (FAQs) about Suicide at **http://www.lib.ox.ac.uk/internet/news/faq/archive/suicide.info.html**

"If you are thinking about suicide . . . read this first" at **http://www.metanoia.org/suicide/**

"Self-Help for Self-Injury" by Anonymous, a personal account of self-mutilation, at **http://www.mindspring.com/~thefly/selfinjury.htm**

Suicide Awareness Voices of Education (SA\VE) at **http://www.save.org/**

Telephone Calls via the Internet—see also Phone Facilitators

Try downloading CoolTalk for Netscape Navigator, or NetMeeting for Microsoft Internet Explorer.

Traumatic Brain Injury

Brain Injury Webring consists "of home pages of Brain Injury Survivors, Caregivers, Friends, Family, and BI

Resources," at **http://www.alliance.net/~jame/bir/bir.htm**

Travel, Trip Planning, and Geographical Information

The Active Traveler Directory of *Outside* Magazine—stay in shape while you travel at **http://outside.starwave.com**

AT&T Travel Directory "can put you in touch with more than 16,000 business providing all-important travel-related services," at **http://att.net/dir800/travdir.html**

CDC—U.S. Government Center for Disease Control and Prevention travel recommendations at **http://www.cdc.gov/**

City.Net allows you to search for information about cities worldwide at **http://www.city.net/**

Doctors' Guide to the Internet at **http://www.pslgroup.com/DOCGUIDE.HTM**

Global Shopping Network Travel Page has a list of airlines' phone numbers and LINKS to a travel agency at **http://www.gsni.com/travel.htm**

Homewood Suites Travel Tips at **http://www.homewood-suites.com/homewooddocs/tips.html**

HotelNet Hotel Finder Service On The Internet at **http://www.hotelnet.co.uk/**

ICOM Travel LINKS at **http://www.icomkorea.com/lvngtogo.html**

Internet Travel Network with low-fare tracker at **http://www.itn.net/cgi/get?itn/index/**

Lonely Planet travel guides, "to kickstart your travels and help you on your way. Just a click away is the latest travel information sourced from our authors, researchers, and fellow travellers," at **http://www.lonelyplanet.com.au/lp.htm**

Medical College of Wisconsin International Travelers' Clinic at **http://www.intmed.mcw.edu/ITC/ITC.html**

PC Travel with LINKS to airline and hotel reservations at **http://www.pctravel.com/**

Route 66, for those who want to travel this historic route, at **http://route66.netvision.be/**

Tourism Offices Worldwide Directory at **http://www.mbnet.mb.ca/lucas/travel/**

Travelocity, "Maximum power for the do-it-yourself traveler," offers trip planning, reservations, and travel information at **http://www.travelocity.com/**

USA City Link at **http://banzai.neosoft.com/citylink/**

Unionization of Mental Health Providers

Federation of Physicians and Dentists, an affiliate of the AFL-CIO, which is interested in representing mental health providers in negotiations with managed care at 1-800-373-5777 and has a Web site at **http://www.nettally.com/fpd/** or e-mail at **rsalinero@nettally.com.**

Usenet Groups Dedicated to Mental Health Issues

WPIC Library is a useful collection of Psychiatry and Psychology Usenet Internet discussion groups. The WPIC page offers three types of groups: (1) alt groups that "present an alternative viewpoint about the subject matter listed . . . usually . . . frequented by people who have a personal interest in the disorder," (2) sci groups, which "discuss scientific research and applications . . . usually oriented toward the professional," and (3) soc groups, which "look at social issues and world cultures." The address of WPIC is **http://wpic.library.pitt.edu/pusenet.htm**

Veronica—see Gopher

Weather Forecast

Intellicast Weather Forecast (U.S. or world) at **http://www.intellicast.com/**

Webrings

I find going in circles around the rings rather tedious but they do contain some valuable links and information.

Home Page of Webrings are "a way to group together sites with similar content (or any pages at all, if one so desires) by linking them together in a circular fashion: a ring," at **http://webring.org**

The Human Mind Webring Home Page "links sites about psychology, psychiatry, emotional and mental health, therapy and counseling," at **http://www.queendom.com/psyring.html**

Webrings related to Health at **http://webring.org/rings_health.html**

White Pages, Phone Directories, and E-Mail Addresses

All Phonebooks Around the World from World Email Directory at **http://worldemail.com//wede4ab.shtml**

CCSO Phonebook Gateway—Server Lookup at
http://www.uiuc.edu/cgi-bin/ph/lookup

College E-Mail Addresses at
http://www.qucis.queensu.ca/FAQs/email/college.html

Four 11 The Internet White Pages ("The most comprehensive and impressive people finder on the Net") offers free Web e-mail, just in case you switch online services, at
http://four11.com/

Infoseek Find People LINKS at
http://www2.infoseek.com/Facts

Netscape's "online white pages provide listings for individuals, but you get an e-mail address instead of a phone number" at
http://home.netscape.com/home/internet-white-pages.html

Switchboard "is becoming synonymous with how people and businesses find each other on the Internet" at
http://www.switchboard.com/

WED World Email Directory "with estimated access to more than 12,000,000 email addresses and more than 140,000,000 business and phone addresses worldwide!" at
http://worldemail.com//

WhoWhere? E-mail Addresses at
http://www.whowhere.com/

WhoWhere? International Phone Directory Links at
http://www.whowhere.com/wwphone/world.html

World Pages People and Business Finder at
http://www.worldpages.com/reshome.html

Windows 95 and Internet Explorer Information

The Microsoft Internet Explorer patch "protects against a security issue discovered by researchers at Princeton" and can be downloaded at **http://www.wnew.com/ie/patch.html**

Windows95.com Windows 95 Information, Drivers, and Shareware at **http://www.windows95.com/**

World Health Organization (WHO)

World Health Organization Home Page at **http://www.who.ch/**

WHO's World Wide Web index, search engines, and other servers at **http://www.who.ch/index/index_servers.html**

Yale Psychiatry Bulletin

Current and graduated members of the Yale University Department of Psychiatry can send announcements about their professional activities to this monthly newsletter. E-mail to **Keppa@aol.com**.

Yellow Pages (just like Ma Bell's) and Toll Free Numbers

AT&T Toll Free Internet Directory of 800 numbers at **http://att.net/dir800/**

AT&T Travel Directory "can put you in touch with more than 16,000 business providing all-important travel-related services" at **http://att.net/dir800/travdir.html**

InfoSpace Yellow Pages at **http://www.infospace.com**

Internet Science, Research, & Technology Yellow Pages at **http://www.iypsrt.com/**

University of Houston College of Business Administration WWW Yellow Pages (this takes a while to load onto your computer): "This site has been awarded four stars by Magellan," at **http://www.cba.uh.edu/yellowptext.html** or **http://www.cba.uh.edu/ylowpges/yb.html**

USA Online, "your online yellow pages for business in the United States of America," at **http://www.usaol.com/index.html**

World Pages E-Mail Search at **http://www.worldpages.com/email.html**

Yellow Pages on the Internet at **http://www.ebp.com/**

Yellow Page Related Sites on the Web at **http://www.wahlstrom.com/ypsites.html**

GLOSSARY OF INTERNET AND COMPUTER TERMS

This glossary contains brief definitions of many Internet-related terms. For the sake of clarity and simplicity, I have included some of the more technical terms here rather than elsewhere in this book. Browsing through this glossary will give you a quick overview of the unique vocabulary of cyberspace. For further details about many of these topics, check out EFF's Extended Guide to the Internet at **http://www.eff.org/papers/eegtti/eeg_toc.html**. Another valuable online resource is the McGraw-Hill Internet Glossary and links to information about the Internet at **http://www.marketing-coach.com/mh-guide/glossary.htm**.

ADDRESS BOOK: An address book is an option of most e-mail programs that allows you to save people's names and e-mail addresses for future reference.

ANALOG: Not digital. Analog information has the form of a continuous flow as in the flow of music or of human speech. Digital information can be broken down into individual units called bits.

ANONYMOUS FTP SERVER: A host/server computer that offers free access to the files on its FTP site. You usually log in to an anonymous FTP site with the user ID *anonymous* and your e-mail address as the password.

ANSI: American National Standards Institute, an organization that sets certain standards for computers.

AOL: America Online, a commercial Internet service provider.

APPLET: A small program written in JAVA computer language. Applets can be incorporated into Web pages and can be safely downloaded and run by your Web browser to provide animation and do other fancy multimedia tricks.

ARCHIE: A search tool used to locate files by name at FTP sites. You must know the exact filename to use Archie.

ARPA: Advanced Research Project Agency of the U.S. Department of Defense. In 1969 Bolt, Beranek, and Newman developed a computer network for ARPA, the ARPANet, which later developed into the Internet. The goal of ARPA-Net was to have a wide area network that could survive a thermonuclear war.

ASCII: American Standard Code Information Exchange refers to the 128 standard keyboard text, numerical, and punctuation symbols that can be read by virtually any computer. The 128 ASCII codes correspond to the hundred and twenty-eight possible 7-digit binary numbers from 0000000 through 1111111 (just as the 64 hexagrams of the Chinese *I Ching* correspond to the sixty-four possible 6-digit binary numbers from 000000 through 111111). E-mail uses ASCII files so that it can be read on any computer in the world. Non-ASCII computer files can only be used by computers similar to the one they were written on.

ASCII ART: "Art" created by combinations of standard keyboard characters. You can Gopher to a collection of ASCII art by typing **gopher://twinbrook.cis.uab.edu/lasciiarc.70** into your Web browser's URL/Address/Location window.

AT&T's WORLDNET: The Internet connection service provided by AT&T. Like AOL, CompuServe, and Sprintnet, Worldnet allows users to connect from just about any location in the United States for the price of a local call.

ATTACHMENT: A file that is transmitted by being attached to an e-mail message. Attached files must be encoded to be able to accompany text-based (ASCII) e-mail and must be decoded by the recipient.

BANDWIDTH: A measure of the amount of data that can be transferred via a connection in a given period of time, often measure in bits per second (bps). Bandwidth is analogous to the diameter of a pipeline that delivers water—the wider the pipe, the more water can flow per second.

BAUD: The rate at which a modem can transfer data is called the baud rate. For purists, baud refers to how many times a carrier signal shifts its value each second. To be strictly accurate, one would say that a 1200 BPS modem runs at 300 baud and moves 4 bits per baud. Thus, 4 bits per baud times 300 baud produces a transfer rate of 1200 bits per second.

BBS: See BULLETIN BOARD SYSTEM.

BINARY FILE: Any computer file that is not an ASCII text file.

BINHEX (BINary HEXidecimal): An encoding method for attaching files to e-mail, used by MacIntosh computers. BinHex converts binary files to ASCII form so they can be sent as e-mail. BinHex coded files must be deBinHexed by the recipient. BinHex is an encoding protocol similar to MIME and UUENCODE.

BIOS: Basic Input/Output System, the group of programs on your computer that enables all its different parts to work together.

BIT: A (B)inary dig(IT), a single unit of information expressed as a bipolar choice between two states such as: on or off, 0 or 1, yes or no, yin or yang, (+) or (–), and so on. Because computers deal with electrical circuits that are either on or off, bits are custom-made for computer information processing. Eight bits in a row make a byte.

BITMAP (BMP): An image made up of numerous little dots. Files containing bitmap images usually end with the extension .bmp.

BITNET: The *Because It's Time Network*, a network of educational sites, is not part of the Internet but is similar to it. Many LISTSERV e-mail discussion groups originated on the Bitnet, and e-mail can be exchanged between the Bitnet and the Internet. Most Bitnet hosts are mainframes that use the VMS operating system. Because of the popularity of the Web on the Internet, the Bitnet network is shrinking as the Internet is growing larger.

BMP: See BITMAP.

BOOKMARK: One of your favorite URLs that Netscape keeps track of so you can go there again.

BOUNCE: An e-mail message bounces back to you when it cannot reach it destination, usually because of an incorrect address.

BPS: Bits per second, a measure of how fast data can flow through a connection. A 14.4 modem can transfer 14,400 bits per second. See BANDWIDTH.

BROWSER (WEB BROWSER): A software program that allows you to access the World Wide Web and read the HTML pages at Web sites (see also CLIENT). Currently, the two most popular browsers are Netscape Navigator and Microsoft Internet Explorer.

BUFFER: Buffering is a way to store information on the computer before using it.

BULLETIN BOARD SYSTEM (BBS): A computer system accessible by modem that offers access to files and often e-mail. Most BBSs are local and gratis. Some companies offer BBSs to customers to provide information and upgrades about products.

BYTE: A sequence typically consisting of eight binary digits (bits) that a computer treats as a unit. Some systems of measurement allow more than eight bits in a byte.

CACHE: After retrieving a Web page, browsers usually store them in a special directory called a cache. The next time you issue a command to retrieve a Web page at a particular URL, the browser will first check to see if it has been stored in the cache. Reading a file from a cache on your own computer is generally much faster than retrieving the same file over the Internet. If the file on the remote computer has changed, you will not know it if the file at that URL has been accessed from the cache on your computer.

CHANNEL: An IRC chat group on the Internet.

CHAT: To correspond with other users interactively online, originally in writing, but now voice chats are available. See also IRC.

CLARINET: You must pay this commercial news service to send you news tailored to your interests via the Internet.

CLIENT: The software that makes uses of the services of a host/server computer on the Internet. For example, the FTP client allows you to download files from FTP sites and the Gopher client presents you with menus of what is available at Gopher sites.

CLIPPER CHIP: A method of encrypting information for secure transmission on the Net. The Clipper Chip has stirred a controversy because only the government would be able to decode the encrypted messages. Cyberpunks refer to the Clipper Chip as the Big Brother or the Wiretap Chip. For more information online, go to the Electronic Frontier Foundation, a nonprofit civil liberties organization, at **http://www.eff.org/**.

COMPRESSION: Compressing a file uses a protocol to shrink a file to a smaller size while preserving the information in that file. Being smaller, compressed files are easier and faster to transmit over the Internet. Compressed files must be decompressed to be restored to their original size and format. A common method of compressing is called ZIP. Zipped files must be unZipped before being used.

COOKIE: A cookie is a small amount of information that the Internet host/server computer sends to your Web browser to store on your hard disk. The host computer then asks for its cookie back the next time you contact that site. Cookies contain data such as your preferences, registration information, sites you have visited, and so on, that the remote computer uses to customize its Web page for you, for example, by sending you a targeted piece of advertising. Many users regard cookies as an intrusion into their privacy. Fortunately, some browsers warn you about cookies and allow you to stop their transmission. Some Web sites will not allow you to view them unless you accept their cookies.

CPU: Central processing unit, the core component or central nervous system of any computer.

CRACKER: A criminal hacker.

CU-SeeMe: A videoconferencing chat utility.

CYBERPUNK: A punk in cyberspace. The term derives from the writings of novelists William Gibson and Bruce Sterling.

CYBERSPACE: A term used by science fiction writer William Gibson to refer to the totality of information available on computer networks and other electronic forms of communication.

DEDICATED LINE: A telephone line that is hard-wired directly to the Internet to allow high-speed transfer of information. Dedicated lines are generally faster and more reliable than dial-up connections.

DIAL-UP: A popular method for connecting to the Internet, using standard telephone lines and a modem to establish a temporary connection between two computers.

DIGERATI: A group of highly computer-literate individuals who are experts on the Net. The term derives from the intellectually elite literati of academia.

DIGEST: A service provided by some mailing lists that make available large groups of messages as a single file. Digests can prevent your e-mail box from being flooded by hundreds of individual messages from the list.

DLL: Dynamic link library. DLL files are usually found in the Windows/System directory and are needed for the functioning of many programs that run under the Windows operating system.

DOMAIN: A region with a unique name on an Internet host/server computer. A host computer connected to the Internet may house several domains. Each host computer has a unique IP address, and each domain has a unique name that parallels the host computer's IP address.

DOMAIN NAME: A unique name that identifies each domain or site on the Internet. Domain names consist of two or more words separated by periods or dots. For example, America Online has the domain name aol.com.

DOMAIN NAME SYSTEM (DNS): DNS is a method for assigning domain names using letters and words corresponding to the unique IP address of the computer that hosts that particular domain.

DOS: Disk Operating System.

DOTTED QUAD: See IP NUMBER.

DOWNLOAD: To download is to transfer a file from a remote computer to your own computer. You must be careful to avoid viruses when downloading.

EASTER EGG: A small, benign program or message that programmers conceal within large applications like Microsoft Word to delight the user who can manage to find it. For more information go to the Web page at **http://www. cnet. com/Content/Features/Howto/Eggs/index.html**.

E-MAIL or ELECTRONIC MAIL: A method of sending messages electronically over the Internet. E-mail is fast and inexpensive, usually the price of a local phone call. E-mail can send only text written with standard keyboard characters (ASCII). Other computer files, however, can be encoded and attached to e-mail messages and then be decoded by the recipient.

EMOTICON: A little text-based graphic design depicting an emotional facial expression like [:-)], which must be viewed by turning one's head to the left horizontally. See also SMILEY.

ENCRYPTION: A method of converting messages into a secret code for purposes of security. Our government is very worried about individuals sending secret messages on the Internet.

ERROR MESSAGE: A message you receive when you make a mistake or a program cannot perform properly. For example, a Web browser might return the error message "404 Not Found" when the requested URL cannot be found on the server. In this case you may have entered the URL incorrectly by misspelling it or not paying attention to case sensitivity. It is also possible that the Web page no longer resides on that server.

ETHERNET: One of the popular methods for linking computers to form a local area network (LAN) to share information.

EUDORA: A sophisticated software program for managing e-mail if you have a direct Internet connection. For useful links to Eudora and other Internet tools, go to **http://www.idiscover.co.uk/links.html**.

FAQ: Frequently asked questions, a document that answers the questions most often asked by users about a particular newsgroup or Internet site.

FAT: File allocation table, a listing of the contents of the directories on a hard disk that enables your computer to know what and where all its files are.

FINGER: A software program that provides identifying information about a user registered at a particular computer. Finger can be used to locate people at an Internet site if that site allows Finger access.

FIREWALL: A combination of hardware and software that prevents unauthorized access to a local computer network (LAN). Firewalls are designed to keep out hackers.

FLAME: To send an insulting, offensive, provocative, or derogatory e-mail message or newsgroup posting.

FLAME WAR: A verbal battle on the Internet of offensive posts and personal attacks.

FREENET: A locally sponsored computer network, often run as a public service by a town or community agency. Access is usually free. You can often download freeware or shareware and have access to e-mail over the Internet.

FREEWARE: Software that is available at no cost. The author retains the copyright and accepts your gratitude as compensation.

FTP (FILE TRANSFER PROTOCOL): A method to connect to an FTP site where you can download files to your own computer. Many host computers maintain anonymous FTP sites as a public service.

FTP SITE: A computer that stores FTP files.

FULLY QUALIFIED DOMAIN NAME (FQDN): The official domain name assigned to a computer.

GATEWAY: A computer system that acts as a go-between to transfer information among or between other computers that use different operating systems.

GENERAL PROTECTION FAULT (GPF): A Windows error message indicating that the program has tried to access an area of memory that is out of the range of memory addresses assigned to it by Windows.

GIF: Graphics interchange format, used to compress and store graphics (picture or image) files.

GIGABYTE (GB): A lot of bytes (about a billion) or exactly, 2 to the 30th power, which equals 1,073,741,824 bytes.

GOPHER: A menu-based tool for locating and retrieving information on the Internet. Gopher originated at the University of Minnesota as a means of tunneling or burrowing through the Internet and presenting you with a menu of what is available. Before the WWW, users relied on Gophers to navigate the Net.

GOPHERSPACE: Gopherspace refers to the totality of all the files available at Gopher sites (or "holes") around the world.

GUI: Graphical user interface, the graphics you see on your monitor.

GUI MUD: (pronounced "gooey mud"). A MUD or multi-user dimension that allows graphics in addition to text. See MUD.

HACKER: A person who devotes huge amounts of time to mastering computer science, programming, and navigating the Internet. Some hackers turn criminal and try to gain unauthorized access to information stored on other people's computers. Hackers who break and enter into other computers are sometimes called crackers. See also PHREAKER.

HOME PAGE (HOMEPAGE): 1) The home page of a Web browser is the page that first appears when you start the browser. 2) Home page also refers to the principal site of an individual or business on the Web. For example, the home page of the Microsoft Corporation lies at **www.microsoft.com**, and from the Microsoft home page you can link to many other Microsoft sites.

HOST: A computer directly connected to the Internet that offers services to other computers on the Net. See also SERVER.

HOTLIST: The Mosaic browser's list of favorite URLs or bookmarks.

HTML: Hypertext markup language, the computer language used for creating documents on the World Wide Web. HTML features hypertext links that allow the Web browser to jump quickly from one Web document to another on computers around the world.

HTTP: Hypertext transfer protocol, which the Internet host computer uses to send Web hypertext documents to your computer. URLs on the Web begin with the name of this protocol (**http://**).

HYPERTEXT: A way to establish links between pages on the World Wide Web. Clicking on a hypertext link will take you to the page to which it is connected on the Web. See also HTML.

ICON: A little image that starts a program or links you to a Web site when you click on it with your mouse.

INTERNET: A worldwide network of computer networks that all use the TCP/IP protocol. An internet (with a small letter i) is formed whenever two or more networks are joined elecronically.

INTERNET PROTOCOL (IP): The computer instructions that regulate how packets of information travel from computer to computer over the Internet.

INTERNET SERVICE PROVIDER (ISP): A service that sells access to the Internet, usually for a monthly fee.

IP ADDRESS: A 32-bit numerical code that uniquely identifies each computer directly connected to the Internet. These numerical codes are sometimes called *dotted quads* and consist of four parts separated by periods or dots (e.g, 207.226.241.14).

IP NUMBER: An IP address (dotted quad) that uniquely identifies each computer directly connected to the Internet.

INTRANET: A private computer network within a business or an organization.

IRC: Internet relay chat, a method for chatting simultaneously with many users worldwide. It originally existed only in text form but now also includes audio. IRC is the Internet equivalent of the CB radio.

ISDN: Integrated services digital network is a special type of telephone line that allows high-speed access to the Internet.

ISP: Internet service provider.

JAVA: An innovative programming language from Sun Microsystems that allows Web browsers to run programs on the Web. Small Java programs called Applets can be included in Web pages to provide animation and other multimedia bells and whistles. Your Web browser can safely download and run these Java Applets while reading a Web page.

JPEG: Joint photographics expert group, a format used to compress and store graphics (picture or image) files.

JUGHEAD: Jughead is a Veronica-like tool that indexes the menus of Gopher sites but allows you to restrict your search to particular regions of Gopherspace.

KBPS: Kilobytes per second, a standard for measuring how fast information is sent over the Internet.

KILOBYTE: One thousand bytes. A thousand kilobytes equals a megabyte.

LEASED LINE: A telephone line that you lease around the clock to connect your computer to one at another site via high-speed Internet (T1 or T3) connections. See T1 and T3.

LISTSERV: A UNIX program that automatically manages e-mail discussions called mailing lists. Typically, you send e-mail to LISTSERV mailing list with the subject header *subscribe listname* (where *listname* is the name of the mailing list). Once subscribed, you will receive by e-mail any new messages posted to the list. Listservs originated on the BITNET network.

LOCAL AREA NETWORK (LAN): A local network of interconnected computers that is confined to a limited area such as a single building. See Wide Area Network.

LOGIN: This refers to the name you use for your account with a particular computer service or system. For example, to login to America Online you must provide your AOL account name. To complete the connection, you must give a valid password. To login to an anonymous FTP site, you usually use the account name *anonymous* and give your e-mail address as the password.

LURK: To enter a chat room simply to observe but not to participate.

LYNX: An early nongraphical, text-based (ASCII) browser for the WWW.

MAILBOMB: A large volume of mail sent to harass a single user. Mailbombing is bad Netiquette.

MAILER-DAEMON: A program that automatically returns incorrectly addressed or otherwise undeliverable mail to its originator.

MAILING LIST: A list of e-mail addresses of people who all receive the mail that is posted to the list. Mailing lists are usually managed by software such as LISTSERV or MAJORDOMO. Mailing lists are like newsgroup discussions, except that messages are sent to your e-mail box rather than maintained on the host computer.

MAJORDOMO: A UNIX program that manages e-mail discussions called mailing lists.

MEGABYTE: One million bytes.

MIDI: Musical instrument digital interface, a method to store musical files and play music on your computer.

MIME: Multipurpose Internet mail extensions, a method for encoding binary files so that they can be sent as attachments to e-mail. MIME is currently becoming the standard encoding protocol.

MIRROR SITE: A site on the Internet that is a mirror image of another site. Mirror sites contain the same content but may be in different languages to make that content more accessible to foreign users. By making FTP files available in several locations, mirror sites can reduce traffic to the original site.

MODEM: MOdulator-DEModulator, a device that allows computers to transfer information over telephone lines. Modems may be internal or external, stationary or portable. Newer modems can transmit and receive faxes on your computer. They can also record voice messages and replace your telephone answering machine.

MODERATED MAILING LIST or NEWSGROUP: A mailing list or newsgroup managed by a human operator who screens messages sent to the list to decide if they are appropriate for distribution to the members of the list.

MOO: This stands for MUD, object oriented, and is a type of multi-user domain for role-playing games. See MUD.

MOSAIC: The first graphical World Wide Web browser which offered access to the WWW, Gopher, FTP, Archie, Usenet newsgroups, WAIS, and Telnet as part of a single software package. Mosaic was developed at the National Center for Supercomputing Applications (NCSA) and is responsible for the current popularity of the Web.

MOUSE: An electronic device used to point and click on items on the computer screen.

MPEG: Motion picture experts group, a format for processing digital audio and video files on your computer.

MUD: Multi-user dungeon (domain, dimension), a text-based virtual environment for role-playing games or for chatting with other users. The MUD games often involve assuming the identity of an imaginary character who interacts with other characters in a fantasy land. You can usually save your character and return to the game the next time you log on. MUD games are highly addictive for some people. MUDs that contain graphics are called GUI MUDs (gooey muds).

MUSE: Multi-user simulated envrionment, a type of MUD, usually without the violence. See MUD.

NETIQUETTE: The rules of etiquette for cyberspace. Generally, one should avoid SHOUTING, spamming, flaming, and the excessive use of emoticons. For more information online, go to **http://www.fau.edu/rinaldi/netiquette.html**.

NETIZEN: A citizen of the Internet.

NETSCAPE: A currently popular Web browser that is based on the Mosaic browser developed at the National Center for Supercomputing Applications (NCSA).

NETWORK: Two or more computers connected electronically to share information and resources.

NEWBIE: A novice on the Internet.

NEWSGROUP: A USENET discussion group, of which there are thousands spanning just about every topic imaginable.

NEWSREADER: Client software that enables you to read newsgroups. Modern Web browsers have built-in newsreaders. Stand-alone newsreaders include Free Agent and NewsWatcher.

NEWS SERVER: A computer that stores newsgroups.

NODE: An individual computer that is part of a network.

ONLINE: A cyberspace adjective meaning that your computer is actively connected to another computer via modem or another connection to the Internet.

OPERATING SYSTEM: A program that your computer needs to operate. Examples of operating systems include UNIX, DOS, and WINDOWS.

PACKET SWITCHING: A method for breaking computer files into small packets of data that can be sent independently over the Internet and then reassembled into exact copies of the original files by the recipient computer. Each packet is labeled with its address of origin and the address of its destination. Since packet switching allows transmission of small packets via any combination of routes along the Net, it obviates the need for a single continuous line connecting the sending and receiving computers.

PASSWORD: A secret code consisting of upper and lower case letters, numbers, and other keyboard characters. Passwords are used for security when attempting access to computer systems. Good passwords are easy for you to remember but almost impossible for someone else to guess. Obvious passwords containing parts of your name, birth date, or address are a hacker's delight.

PCMCIA: This stands for Personal Computer Memory Card Industry Association, a developer of very portable devices like modems for laptop computers.

PERMANENT CONNECTION: A permanent connection, as the name implies, involves a dedicated high-speed line or cable that connects your computer directly to the Internet twenty-four hours a day.

PHREAKER: A person who breaks into telephone systems to steal calling card numbers and/or make free long-distance calls.

PLUG-IN: A program that electronically "plugs into" your Web browser and enhances its capabilities. For example, plug-ins allow you to listen to real time audio or to view video clips.

POINT OF PRESENCE (PoP): A point of presence is a location (like a city) where you can connect to the Internet via your Internet service provider.

POINT-TO-POINT PROTOCOL (PPP): one of the standard dialup protocols (like the older SLIP) for connecting to the Internet via TCP/IP and sending packets of information over serial lines like telephone lines and RS-232 cables. The PPP protocol allows you to use Internet software like Web browsers over regular telephone lines. PPP is more reliable than SLIP because it checks to be sure the transmission is free of errors.

POST, POSTING: A message sent to a newsgroup or mailing list.

POST OFFICE PROTOCOL (POP): The post office protocol

is the method your e-mail software uses to retrieve and send your e-mail.

PRETTY GOOD PRIVACY (PGP): A method for encrypting e-mail. The government is opposed to PGP because the code is so difficult to crack. See CLIPPER CHIP.

PROTOCOL: A set of rules that set standards for how computers operate or communicate. Protocols allow computers of different types to share information and resources.

QUICKTIME: Apple's video format, which uses .mov files.

REALAUDIO: A method invented by Rob Glasser to play sound files from sites on the Internet. By utilizing a buffer, RealAudio allows sound files to be played without first completely downloading the file.

ROTATE 13 (ROT 13): A method for encrypting newsgroups messages.

ROUTER: A specialized computer that directs traffic on the Internet, much the same way as a central post office directs the flow of paper mail. Routers follow instructions laid out in routing protocols.

SEARCH ENGINE: A program that searches for Internet sites by keywords and often by key phrases. AltaVista and Webcrawler are popular search engines.

SECURE HYPERTEXT TRANSFER PROTOCOL (SHTTP): A method of encryption for the Web.

SECURE SOCKETS LAYER: See SSL.

SERVER: A computer directly connected to the Internet that serves the other computers attached to it. Server computers are also called HOSTS. In addition, the term refers to the software that runs on a host computer to provide service to its clients.

SERVICE PROVIDER: A commercial enterprise that sells its users access to the Internet, usually for a monthly fee.

SHAREWARE: Software that is available free for trial usage. If you like the software and continue to use it, you are honor-bound to pay its author. Some shareware programs cease functioning within thirty days if you don't pay up. A good site from which to search for shareware is **http://www.shareware.com/**.

SHELL ACCOUNT: Instead of having your own direct Internet connection, you can gain access through a shell account that lets you connect to the Internet by first connecting to a host computer that allows you to use its direct connection to the Internet.

SHOUT: The use of all capital letters in posts on the Internet.

SIGNATURE FILE: An ASCII text file that contains your identifying information for inclusion as your "signature" at the end of an e-mail message.

SLIP: Serial line Internet protocol, one of the older standard dialup protocols (like the newer PPP) for connecting to the Internet via TCP/IP over serial lines like telephone lines and RS-232 cables. CSLIP is the same as SLIP but the data is compressed for quicker transmission.

SMILEY: A little text-based graphic design depicting a facial expression like :-(,which must be viewed by turning one's head to the left horizontally. Smileys are a type of EMOTICON.

SPAM: Unwanted, junk postings that are widely distributed to individuals, mailing lists, or newsgroups on the Net.

SPRINTNET: The Internet connection service provided by Sprint. Like AOL, CompuServe, and Worldnet, Sprintnet allows users to connect from just about any location in the United States for the price of a local call.

SSL (SECURE SOCKETS LAYER): The method used by Netscape Communications to encrypt and send messages or confidential information securely on the Internet. Using SSL, both the sender and receiver exchange security certificates that allow them and no one else to decode the encrypted messages.

SUBSCRIBE: To sign up for a mailing list by sending a request to the administrative e-mail address of the list.

SYSOP: System operator, the person responsible for managing a resource on the Internet. If you violate the rules of a resource, you may get an e-mail from the sysop or you may be denied further access.

T1 and T3: Types of very high-speed leased-line computer connections for the Internet.

TCP/IP: Transmission control protocol/Internet protocol, the software instructions (protocol) that make possible the accurate transfer of information on the Internet.

TDD/TTY: Tone Dialing for Deaf/Teletype, a method that enables the hearing-impaired to send messages on phone lines.

TELNET: Software that allows your computer to act like a terminal connected to a remote host computer. Using Telnet, you can login to the remote computer and use many of its services. When you Telnet to a remote computer, you typically need to login and provide a password to gain entry.

TERMINAL: A device consisting minimally of a monitor, keyboard, simple circuitry, and its software, for connecting to and using resources on a remote computer. Telnet allows your home computer to act like a dumb terminal to a remote site.

THREAD: A series of Usenet newsgroup messages or articles that all deal with the same topic. Threads usually begin with an article that several members of the discussion group respond to or comment about.

TWAIN: Technology without an interesting name, a standard used in scanners.

UNIFORM RESOURCE LOCATOR: See URL.

UNIX: An operating system (like DOS), developed by AT&T, that allows one host computer to service many clients simultaneously. Many host computers on the Internet use the UNIX operating system. For a brief introduction to UNIX, read the article "Seven UNIX Commands You Can't Live Without" at **http://www.eff.org/papers/eegtti/eeg_64.html**.

UNMODERATED MAILING LIST or NEWSGROUP: A mailing list or newsgroup managed automatically by computer software. All messages sent to the list are automatically distributed to the members without censorship.

UNSUBSCRIBE: The opposite of SUBSCRIBE.

UPLOAD: To upload is to send a file from your computer to a remote computer.

URL: Uniform resource locator, a method for specifying addresses on the Internet (like a ZIP-plus-4 code for the Internet). A typical URL on the Web looks like this: **http://DomainName/directory/filename**.

USENET: User's Network, a computer network containing a large collection of test-based files organized by topic into various newsgroups.

USER ID: An identifying name that you use to log on to your account with an Internet service provider.

USER-TO-LINE RATIO: The ratio of the number of users to the number of telephone lines made available by an Internet service provider. The industry standard is 12 to 15 users per phone line. Anything above 15 to 1 is likely to result in frequent busy signals when you try to log on.

UUENCODE: UNIX to UNIX encoding, a method for encoding binary files on UNIX systems so that they can be sent as attachments to e-mail. Basically, UUENCODE converts DOS and UNIX binary (non-ASCII) files into ASCII files that can travel by e-mail. Such files must be UUDECODED by the recipient.

VERONICA: Veronica (Very Easy Rodent Oriented Net-wide Index of Computerized Archives) is a UNIX-based tool that indexes the menus of all the Gophers in the world, making it possible to locate a particular Gopher hole that contains the information you are seeking.

VIRTUAL OBJECT: The three-dimensional image of an object on your monitor. You can move around a three-dimensional object to view it from different angles on your screen.

VIRTUAL REALITY or VIRTUAL WORLDS: The world of three-dimensional images available via 3-D browsers that can interpret VRML programming language. You can find a 3-D browser at Plug-In Plaza on the Web at **http://browserwatch.iworld.com/plug-in.html**.

VIRUS: A virus is a nasty little computer program that transfers from computer to computer via modem or floppy disks. Viruses "infect" the computer's hard disk, replicate, and spread to other computers, often causing damage in their wake. No computer should be without a good virus checker and remover. Check out the Anti-Virus Update Center at **http://www.crl.com/%7Ecolocomp/novirus2.htm**.

VRML: Virtual reality modeling language, used for creating 3-D images that can be viewed with a 3-D browser like WebSpace and WebFX. See VIRTUAL REALITY.

VT100: A terminal emulation mode used by many remote computers. You may be asked to choose a terminal emulation mode when you use Telnet to connect to a host computer.

WAIS: Wide area information server. WAIS allows keyword searches of databases of Web pages and returns a list of documents ranked according to how often the keywords appear. Many Web search engines use WAIS technology.

WAN: Wide area network.

WAV: Microsoft's WAVeform sound format for encoding sound files.

WEB BROWSER: See BROWSER.

WEBMASTER or WEBMISTRESS: A person who manages a Web site.

WEB PAGE: A hypertext document on the World Wide Web. Each Web page has a unique URL address.

WEB SITE: A computer that stores Web pages.

WEBSPACE: The name of a popular 3-D browser that can interpret VRML programming language and display 3-D images on your screen.

WHITE PAGES: Netscape's Internet directory, containing many e-mail addresses at **http://home.netscape.com/home/internet-white-pages.html**.

WHOIS: This is an Internet tool that returns identifying information about who is in charge of a host computer when you enter its domain name.

WIDE AREA NETWORK (WAN): Any network of interconnected computers that spans an area larger (wider) than a single building or a single college campus.

WINDOWS: Microsoft's immensely popular graphical user interface program that has replaced their DOS operating system.

WINSOCK: Winsock is short for Windows Socket and refers to the rules and standards for computer programs that allow TCP/IP Internet connections on a Windows system. The Winsock program allows you to run your browser and other Internet applications on your computer. When you install TCP/IP Internet software, it usually places a file called winsock.dll in the Windows/system directory. If you install two different Internet connection software packages, you may have two different winsock.dll files and conflicts may arise.

WINVN: A stand alone newsgroup reader for Windows systems.

WORLD WIDE WEB (WWW): The Web, which originated at CERN in Switzerland, is a huge collection of Internet documents, connected by hypertext links and viewed via a Web browser like Mosaic, Netscape Navigator, or Microsoft Internet Explorer. The host computer sends Web documents to your computer via the hypertext transfer protocol (http). Web documents can link to text, graphics, sound, and other types of multimedia files.

WORLDS CHAT: A popular 3-D chat program available at **http://www.worlds.net**, in which you can select a three-dimensional object to represent yourself as you wander through a virtual world on the Net.

WPG: WordPerfect graphics.

WYSIWYG: What you see is what you get, a feature of word processors and Web editors that allows you to see how a page will actually look, based on the text and commands that you write.

YAHOO: A popular database of Web sites that can be searched by keywords. It is available at **http://www.yahoo.com**.

ZIP: Zone information protocol is a popular method of file compression, useful for the rapid transmission of files across the Internet.

BIBLIOGRAPHY

Burns, J. (1996). *Glossary of Computer/Internet Terms.* WWW: **http://www.htmlgoodies.com**.

Clark, D. (1996). *Student's Guide to the Internet, Second Edition.* Indianapolis, IN: Que Corporation.

CRT Multimedia Software (1996). *Easy Tutor Get Connected 96, CD Version 1.1.*

Dilger, P. (1997). Bigots cast a wider Net—The Web's an inviting place for hate groups. *The New Haven Register*, March 16, p. 1.

Flynn, L. J. (1997). Just drive a used PC off the lot and save. *The New York Times*, February 23, Section 3, p. 10.

Gaffin, A., and Heitkötter, J. (1994). *EFF's Extended Guide to the Internet.* WWW: **http://www.eff.org/papers/eegtti/eeg_ toc.html**.

Greenhouse, L. (1997). High court weighs decency-act case. *The New York Times*, March 24, p. D5.

Hahn, H. (1997). *Internet & Web Yellow Pages, 1997 Edition.* Berkeley, CA: Osborne/McGraw-Hill.

Huang, K., and Huang, R. (1987). *I Ching.* New York: Workman.

Internet Literacy Consultants (1997). *ILC Glossary of Internet Terms.* WWW: **http://www.matisse.net/files/glossary.html**.

Kennedy, A. J. (1995). *The Internet et World Wide Web.* London: Rough Guides, Ltd. (**http://roughguides.com/**).

Krol, E., and Ferguson, P. (1995). *The Whole Internet For Windows 95.* Sebastopol, CA: O'Reilly & Associates.

Maran Graphics (1995). *Internet and World Wide Web Simplified.* Foster City, CA: IDG Books.

Markoff, J. (1997). New software expected to cut web delays. *The New York Times*, February 17, p. 42.

Maurer, K. (1996). Internet 'addiction' surfs into therapists' offices. *Clinical Psychiatry News* 24:10.

Nelson, J. (1996). *The Internet Tutor.* WWW: **http://www.i-tutor.com/**.

Newsweek (1997). Internet U—no ivy, no walls, no keg parties. March 10, p. 12.

PC Novice Guide to the Web (1996). Lincoln, NE: Peed Corporation.

Romm, D. (1996). *The Jewish Guide to the Internet.* Northvale, NJ: Jason Aronson.

Rosenberg, G. (1997). Electronic discovery proves an effective legal weapon, looking for evidence in discarded e-mail. *The New York Times*, March 31, p. D5.

Rowland, R., and Kinnaman, D. (1995). *Researching on the Internet.* Rocklin, CA: Prima Publishing.

Schetky, D. (1997). New communication methods pose new privacy dangers. *Connecticut Psychiatrist* 38:1, p. 5.

Suarez, P. J. (1995). *Beginners Guide to the Internet. Release 2.0.* Miamisburg, OH: Suarez Associates.

Sweeney, D. (1997). Dialing for data. *Mobile Computing and Communications*, March, pp. 56–64.

Wagner, R. L., and Engelmann, E. (1996). *The McGraw-Hill Internet Training Manual.* New York: McGraw-Hill.

INDEX

Abuse, sites about, 100–101
Addictions, sites about, 101
Addresses
  for e-mail, 46–47, 55
  for FTP sites, 65–68
Advanced Research Projects Agency (ARPA), and packet-switching technology, 28–29
Advertising, on Juno e-mail service, 54–55
AIDS, sites about, 102–103
AltaVista (search engine), 87–88
Alternative mental health, sites about, 136–138
Alzheimer's disease, sites about, 103
America Online (AOL)
  home pages through, 93
  signing onto, 42–43
  subscriber backlogs, 39–40
  Web browser on, 80
American Civil Liberties Union, sites about, 103
American Psychological Association, sites about publication style, 104
Analog, *vs.* digital, 21
Analysis, Jungian, sites about, 127
Angelfire, Web page editor, 32, 93
Anonymous FTP sites, 65
Anxiety disorders, sites about, 104, 106
APA publication style, sites about, 104
Archie
  program for finding FTP files, 70
  sites about, 104
Articles, attached to e-mail, 3–4
ASCII
  art, 48–49
  e-mail translated into, 50–51
  Gopher files in, 71
ASCII art, 48–49
Attachments, to e-mail, 3–4, 46, 50–52
Attention Deficit Hyperactivity Disorder (ADHD), sites for, 106

Back up, as virus protection, 26
Banking, on the Web, 14–15

Batteries
  for back up, 24
  for portable modems, 23
Berners-Lee, Tim, and World Wide Web, 77
Bigfoot, maintaining same e-mail address through, 55
Billing, electronic, 12–13
Binary system, 20
  attachments to e-mail in, 50
  in packet-switching technology, 31–32
Bipolar disorder, sites about, 113–114
Bookmarks, for favorite Web pages, 83, 88
Books, sites about, 106–107, 109
Boolean searches, 87–88
Brain, sites about, 136, 158–159
Bulletin board system, Internet access through, 41–42

Cable modems, 22
Cache, on hard disk, 82, 88
Callahan Online, 86–87
Carbon copies, of e-mail, 2, 48–50
Censorship
  of children's access, 92
    sites about, 140–141
  of Internet, 16–18
CERN, and World Wide Web, 77
Chat rooms, 4–6. *See also* Mailing lists; Newsgroups
  pornography and hate groups in, 16–18, 92
  sites for, 107
Children
  and Internet pornography, 16–18, 92
  parental guidance sites, 140–141
Clipper Chip, 91
Commands, for e-mail, 52–53
CompuServe, signing onto, 42–43
Computers
  development of personal, 30
  in mental health, sites about, 107, 108
Confidentiality
  lack of, in e-mail, 12–13, 53–54
  and monitoring of computer communications, 18
Continuing education, 11
  sites about, 108–109
Copyright information, sites for, 109
Cyberspace, regions in, 63–64

Databases
  for finding people, 12
  searches of, 11
  sites for, 109–113, 148
  for Usenet newsgroups, 6–7
  Web directories as, 149–152

Death, sites about, 113
Depression, sites about, 113–114
Diagnosis, sites about, 114
Dictionaries
  sites for, 115–116
  sites for Internet glossaries, 121–122
Digests, for mailing lists, 56
Digital Subscriber Lines (xDSL), as alternative to modems, 22
Digitalization, 20
Directories
  of e-mail addresses, 46–47, 161–162
  of fax numbers, 10, 117
  of FTP sites, 65–68
  Gopherspace, 70–72
  of mental health providers, 134–135
  phone, 12
    international, 10
    toll-free, 163–164
    white pages, 161–162
    yellow pages, 163–164
  Web
    events, 119
    pages and Internet resources, 99–164
    search engines, 84–88
    sites about, 149–152
  zip codes, etc., 12
Disabilities, sites about, 114
Discussion groups about mental health, sites for, 114–115
DNS (domain name system), and URL addresses, 35–37
Documents, attached to e-mail, 3–4, 46, 50–52
Domain names
  as IP addresses, 32–34
  and URL addresses, 35–37
Dreams, sites about, 156
DSM-IV, sites about, 114

Eating disorders, sites about, 115
Educational resources, sites about, 115–116, 141–142
Electrical fluctuations, surge protection against, 24
Electronic billing, 12–13
E-mail, 3–4, 30, 45–55
  addresses for
    directories of, 161–162
    IP, 32–34
    maintaining same, 55
  attachments to, 3–4, 46, 50–52
  combined with faxing, 10
  commands for, 52–53
  free, 42, 54–55, 119–120
  lack of confidentiality in, 12–13, 53–54
  mailing lists through, 42, 55–58
  phone facilitators for, 143–144

E-mail (*continued*)
reasons to use, 2
through Web browsers, 83
for Usenet newsgroups, 6–7
Emoticons, 48–49
avoiding use of, 61
Employment, sites about, 123
Encoding, of attachments to e-mail into binary, 50–51
Encryption, 91
Entertainment, on the Web, 15–16
Equipment, for voice and video conferencing, 8
Exon/Gorton Communications Decency Act of 1996, 16–17
External modems, 23

FAQ (frequently asked questions) documents, 47
of newsgroups, 61
Faxing, 10
directories of numbers, 10, 117
modems for, 24
Feldman, Joan, on confidentiality of e-mail, 54
File extensions, for FTP sites, 68–69
Files
attached to e-mail, 3–4, 46, 50–52
downloading, 9–10
and virus protection, 25–26
from FTP sites, 65–70
types and extensions, 68–69
zipping, 50–52
Finances
electronic billing, 12–13
personal, 14–15
sites about, 117
Finger
finding information on users with, 74
sites about, 104, 117
Flaming, 32
avoiding, 61
Forensic psychiatry, sites about, 117–118
Freeware
anti-virus, 26
downloading, 9–10
FTP (file transfer protocol) sites
downloading programs and files from, 10, 65–70
sites about, 104, 118
virus protection in, 26
Fun, on the Web, 15–16

Gates, Bill, paranoia about, 18
Geographical information, sites for, 159–160
Gopher, 30
catalogs of menus of, 72
for finding FTP information, 70–72
and search for e-mail addresses, 46
sites about, 118–119

Government
  eavesdropping by, 18
  opposition to encryption, 91
Grants, sites for, 118
Graphics, in Web browsers, 79–81, 83–84
Grieving, sites about, 113

Handles
  for e-mail, 46
  for IRC (Internet Relay Chat), 6
HIV, sites about, 102–103
Hoffman, Michelle, on Web browser plug-ins, 90
Holistic mental health, sites about, 136–138
Home pages
  creating, 92–98
  free, 5, 13–14, 119–120
  mIRC, 6
  for Web browsers, 82, 85
Homosexuality, sites about, 153–155
Host computers, 3, 38–41
  accessing files of, 65
  finding information on, 74
  in IP addresses, 32–33
  and Telnet, 73
Hypermedia, links on World Wide Web, 35
Hypertext, 80–81
  on World Wide Web, 35, 77–78
Hypertext markup language (HTML)
  in creating home pages, 92–98
  sites about, 120–121
  source code for Web browsers, 84
  in World Wide Web, 78
Hypertext transfer protocol (http), 78
  in URL addresses, 35–37

I Ching, 20
IBM, *vs.* Macintosh, in FTP sites, 67
Institutions, type of, in IP addresses, 33–34
Integrated Services Digital Network (ISDN), as alternative to modems, 22
Internal modems, 23
International correspondence
  e-mail combined with faxing, 10
  IP addresses for, 33–34
  through IRC, 5–6
Internet, 1–2
  access to, 30
  addresses on
    changing of, 3, 100
    IP, 32–34
  checking connections with Ping, 74–75

Internet (*continued*)
competition by Microsoft Network, 18
development of, 2–3, 28–30
and modem speed, 21–22
old tools for, 63–75, 78
phone company charges for, 8–9
sites for information about, 121–122
structure of, 27
tutorials for, 11
Internet access providers (IAPs). *See* Internet service providers (ISPs)
Internet Radio, 7
Internet Relay Chat (IRC), 5–6
Internet service providers (ISPs), 38–44
phone company charges for, 8–9
sites about, 121
types of connections for, 43
IP (internetworking protocol), 29, 31–32
IRC (Internet Relay Chat), 5–6

Java, 90–91
Job hunting
sites about, 123
on the Web, 15
Journals, sites about, 123–127
Jughead, catalog of Gopher menus, 72
Jungian psychology, sites about, 127
Juno, free e-mail service, 54–55

Kennedy, A. J., on Microsoft, 18
Keywords
with search engines, 99
in searches with WAIS, 73–74

Leibniz, Gottfried Wilhelm von, 19–20
Libraries
accessed via Telnet, 73
searches of, 11
sites for, 115–116, 128
Links among mental health resources, sites about, 128–130
Literature searches, 11
through CompuServe, 43
Login IDs, for Telnet, 73
Lynx (old Web browser), 79

Macintosh, *vs.* IBM, in FTP sites, 67
Macro viruses, 25
Mailing lists
compared to newsgroups, 60
sites about, 130
through e-mail, 42, 55–58
Managed care, sites about, 131
quality rankings of, 148
Mardam-Bey, Khaled, 6
Medicaid, sites about, 132

Medical resources, sites about, 131–132
  World Health Organization, 163
Medicare, sites about, 132
Medications, sites about, 133–134
Meditation, sites about, 157–158
MedLine, 11
  free searches, 134
Mental health sites
  alternative, 136–138
  computers in, 107, 108
  databases for, 109–113
  discussions, 114–115
  links among resources in, 128–130
  patient education, 141–142
  providers
    directory of, 134–135
    unionization of, 160
  questions about, 105–106
  usenet groups about, 160–161
Menus, through Gopher, 70–72
Microsoft, 30
activism against phone company fee increases, 8–9
  and macro viruses, 25
  paranoia about, 18
Microsoft Internet Explorer (Web browser), 38, 78, 79–80
  features of, 7, 81–84
  plug-ins for, 89–90
  sites about, 163
Microsoft Network, 18, 30
  and local access numbers, 39–40
Military, and packet-switching technology, 28–29
Modems
  and digitalization for phone lines, 20–21
  speed of, 21–22
  types of, 22–24
  voice-capable, 4
Mosaic (Web browser), 78–80

Netiquette, 33
  for mailing lists, 58
  for newsgroups, 60–61
Netscape Navigator (Web browser), 7, 38, 78, 79–80
  plug-ins for, 89
Networks, and Internet structure, 27
Neurology, sites about, 135–136
Neuropsychology, sites about, 136
New age mental health, sites about, 136–138
News
  commercial, 7–8
  online, 138–140
Newsgroups, 6–7, 30, 58–61, 138
  compared to mailing lists, 60
  through Web browsers, 83
Newspapers, online, 138–140
Nursing, sites about, 140

Obsessive compulsive disorder, sites about, 140
Oikarinen, Jarkko, 5–6
Online services, 30, 43–44
  cautions about, 39–41
  chat rooms of, 4–5
  free home pages by, 13–14
  Internet access from, 38

Packets, routing for, 31, 39
Packet-switching technology, 28–29
  and IPs, 31
Panic disorders, sites about, 104, 106
Parental guidance, censorship of children's access, 17–18
  sites about, 140–141
Passwords, 12
  for FTP sites, 65
  for Telnet, 73
Patient education, 12–13
  sites about, 141–142
PCMCIA modems, 23–24
PCs (personal computers), development of, 30
People locator sites, 12, 143. *See also* Directories
Phobic disorders, sites about, 104
Phone. *See* Telephone
Physicians Online (POL) Network, 144
Ping, tool to check Internet connections, 74–75
Plug-ins, for Web browsers, 89–90
Pornography
  Internet, 16–18, 92
  and parental guidance sites, 140–141
Portable modems, 23–24
Pretty Good Privacy (encryption program), 12–13, 91
Privacy
  in e-mail
    encryption utility, 12–13
    lack of, 53–54
  on the Web, 91–92
Professional association sites, 144–146
Programs
  downloading, 9–10
    and virus protection, 25–26
  running on host computers via Telnet, 73
  to translate encoding protocols, 50–51
Psychiatry, Yale Bulletin site, 163
Psychoanalysis, sites about, 146
Psychology, sites about
  history, 119
  Jungian, 127
  links to sources within, 147
  testing and screening, 146–147

Psychopharmacology, sites about, 133–134
Psychotherapy sites, 147
Publishing, sites about, 106–107
Punctuation, in URL addresses, 35–37

Questions
FAQ documents, 47, 61
for Usenet newsgroups, 6–7

Radio, Internet, 7, 138–140
Rape, sites about, 100–101
README files, 66–67
Reference, sites about research tools, 148
Refresh command, 82, 84
Research
of databases, literature, and libraries, 11
literature search through CompuServe, 43
sites for, 148
Web directories, 149–152
travel planning, 14
Research funding, sites about, 118
Robots, for Web search engines, 85
Routers, 31, 39

Schetksy, Diane, on lack of privacy in e-mail, 54
Schizophrenia, sites about, 149
Search engines, 99
sites about, 149–152
gophers, 118–119
Web, 84–88
Searches
Medline, 134
sites for, 104–105
people locators, 143
with WAIS, 73–74
Security. *See also* Confidentiality
and packet-switching technology, 28–29
for the Web, 15, 91–92
Self-help, sites about, 152–153
stress management, 157–158
Self-mutilation, sites about, 158
Servers, 38–41
and e-mail addresses, 46
IRC, 6
Service providers. *See* Internet service providers (ISPs)
Sexuality, sites about, 153–155
Shareware
anti-virus, 26
downloading programs, 9–10
for FTP files, 69
sites about, 155–156
Shopping, on the Web, 14
sites about, 155
Shouting, 32–33
avoiding, 61

Sleep issues, sites about, 156
Snail mail, 2, 45–46
Social work, sites about, 156–157
Software
  anti-virus, 26
  for downloading programs and files, 9–10
  e-mail, 48–50
  for finding FTP files, 70
  for Internet providers, 41
  for Internet Radio, 7–8
  for mailing lists, 56
  servers, 38–41
  for smart telephones, 4
  for voice and video conferencing, 8
  for zipping files, 52
Source code, for Web browsers, 84
Spamming, 32
  avoiding, 61
Spanish language and culture, sites about, 157
Spiders, for Web search engines, 85
Stress management, sites about, 157–158
Suicide prevention, sites about, 158
Support groups, 11, 15–16
  sites about, 101–102, 152–153
Surge protection, 24
Survivors, abuse, sites about, 100–101

TCP (transmission control protocol), 31
Technical support, for Internet providers, 41
Telephone companies, charges for Internet access by, 8–9, 38, 39–40
Telephone facilitators, e-mail, 143–144
Telephones
  calls via Internet, 158
  digitalization for, 20–21
  directories, 12, 161–162
    international, 10
    yellow pages and toll-free, 163–164
  and modem speed, 21–22
  phone facilitators, 143–144
  smart, for e-mail, 4
Telnet, 73
  sites for, 104
Templates, e-mail, 48–50
Tourette's Syndrome, sites about, 140
Transmission control protocol (TCP), 31
Trauma, sites about, 100–101
  brain injury, 158–159
Travel planning, 14
  sites about, 159–160
Trolling, avoiding, 61

Tutorials
  Internet, 11
    sites about, 121–122
  on Web browser plug-ins, 90

Unionization, in mental health, sites about, 160
Unix, 13
  as alternative to FTP, 65
  finger command from, 74
URL (uniform resource locator) addresses, 35–37
  changing of, 100
  for FTP sites, 65–68
  keeping updated, 88
  for newsgroups, 58
URL-Minder, notification of changes to Web pages, 89
Usenet, 138
  mental health sites on, 160–161
  newsgroups on, 6–7, 58–59

Veronica, catalog of Gopher menus, 72
Video conferencing, 8–9
Videos, attached to e-mail, 3–4
Viruses, 24–26
  avoiding, 10
  sites about, 108
Voice conferencing, 8–9

WAIS (Wide Area Information Server), 30
  searches with, 73–74
WBS (WebChat Broadcasting System), 5
Weather forecasts, 161
Web browsers, 13–14, 30, 78–79
  accessing newsgroups through, 58
  e-mail forms in, 48–50
  graphical, 79–84
  Internet tools in, 63
  plug-ins for, 89–90
  as server software, 38
Web Buddy (search engine assistant), 88
Web pages
  editors for, 92–93
  notification of changes to, 88
  personal, 82–83
Webcrawler (search engine), 86
Webrings, 161
Whois, 74
Windows 95, 163
  and Internet set up, 43
  Microsoft Network in, 18
World Health Organization (WHO) site, 163
World Wide Web, 13–14, 77–99
  addresses on
    directory sites, 149–152
    IP, 32–34
    URL, 35–36
  changes on, 100
    speed of, 82, 85
  development of, 30

World Wide Web (*continued*)
FTP sites on, 67
reasons to use, 2–3
security on, 91–92
Worms, for Web search engines, 85

XDSL, as alternative to modems, 22

Yahoo, Web search engines, 86–87
Yale Psychiatry Bulletin site, 163
Yin and yang, and binary numbers, 19–20

Zimmerman, Phil, 12–13
Zipping files, 51–52

ABOUT THE AUTHOR

Anthony L. LaBruzza, M.D., a psychiatrist, is Chief of Medicine and Medical Director of the Community Services Division at the Greater Bridgeport Community Mental Health Center in Bridgeport, Connecticut. He is a member of the clinical faculty of the Yale School of Medicine and was a site coordinator for the *DSM-IV* General Reliability Field Trial. Dr. LaBruzza received a master's degree in mathematics from Fordham University and an M.D. from the Albert Einstein College of Medicine. He was trained in psychiatry at Yale and also attended the Western New England Institute for Psychoanalysis, both in New Haven.